THE PRESIDENT, THE PROFESSOR,
AND THE COLLEGE LIBRARY

By the same author

THE ADMINISTRATION OF THE COLLEGE LIBRARY

The President the Professor and the College Library

BY GUY R. LYLE
DIRECTOR OF LIBRARIES
EMORY UNIVERSITY

With an introductory chapter
BY KEVIN GUINAGH

THE H. W. WILSON COMPANY
NEW YORK   1963

TO

RUTH

TOM

EVAN

for their wit,
assistance,
and encouragement

Author's Note

THE THREE TALKS contained herein were given at library conferences in 1961 and 1962. All three were addressed to librarians but they called attention to library problems in which college administrators and faculty have a primary stake if they wish to put their libraries to the most effective use. A number of the persons present at the meetings were kind enough to suggest that the talks would serve a useful purpose if they were printed and made easily available to college presidents and professors.

Librarians can manage their problems of acquisition and cataloging, of housing and distributing books, of assigning spaces and personnel with little more than financial assistance from the college. But in order to participate fully in the process of education, to build fine collections, and to encourage students to use library materials extensively and wisely, they must have the full cooperation of college administrators and the faculty. These three topics are roughly the subjects of the talks. They cannot be treated independently because they run into one another, but I have not attempted to weld them together in any way. Instead,

I have ventured to add a brief final chapter which offers a blue-print of some of the problems that need to be faced frankly by administrators and faculty if the library is to be an effective means of college instruction.

Since it is quite uncommon for a college librarian to speak directly to an audience of presidents and professors, I have asked Dr. Kevin Guinagh, Department of Foreign Languages, Eastern Illinois University, to act as my go-between. His introductory chapter, "The Academic Image of the Librarian," is a heartening salute to the library profession.

GUY R. LYLE

Atlanta, Georgia
October 15, 1962

Table of Contents

Author's Note 7

The Academic Image of the Librarian, by Kevin Guinagh .. 11

The College Administration and the Library 20

Developing the College Library Book Collection 34

Use and Misuse of the College Library 51

Blueprint for a College Library 58

Appendix

    Survey of Library Use 73

    Accredited Library Schools—American Library Association 74

    Standards for College Libraries 76

Index 87

The Academic Image of the Librarian

An introductory chapter by
KEVIN GUINAGH

THE POPULARITY of different academic departments in a college is rarely stable for a long period of time. Interest in different areas is always rising and falling. At the moment, thanks to the scientific advances of our national enemies, there is great interest in physical science, mathematics, and foreign languages; in fact, interest is so great in these areas that the Government is paying teachers of these subjects to go to school for additional training. Not long ago guidance experts were waving students away from these studies with the warning that they would find themselves among the unemployed after graduation because there would be a lessening demand for persons competent in these fields.

There was a time in the history of scholarship—we must go back to ancient Alexandria to spot the peak—when librarians were treated with the highest respect. They had the ear of the mighty; they were considered the custodians of learning. Today, however, many librarians say that they are not appreciated by the academic community. They feel that they are psychologically and physically isolated. Like the rest of mankind, librarians cherish a desire to be understood. If they were given the opportunity to explain themselves, they feel, administrators and professors would understand them and applaud their contributions to the intellectual life of the college.

This feeling on the part of the librarians that they are not appreciated is by no means the groundless reaction of a few hypersensitive individuals. There is a basis for this conviction. Recently a professor was heard to disapprove of the practice of giving sabbatical leaves to librarians. When a colleague expressed surprise that he should regard such intelligent and devoted members of his college staff as second class citizens or even Janizaries, he cited with evident approval the practice prevalent in his alma mater of treating them as clerks.

Such professors keep alive certain myths about librarians. The first of these runs to the effect that the happy librarian is one who has all the books in the library catalog neatly shelved and dusted. He is pictured as a heavily armed miser blocking the only entrance to the stacks. Very likely those who cultivate this myth have had some words with a librarian who insisted that the library rules must be observed. Some few professors whom even administrators fear to cross must sometimes be told that the rules must be obeyed. One of the less pleasant phases of the librarian's work may be an occasional bout with an indignant professor who feels his position is not appreciated.

Any reader who has observed college library practice recently or who has read just a little in library journals realizes that the policy of modern librarians is to put books into the hands of patrons. They often set up attractive displays of books on current problems or on general cultural themes in which they feel the college community should be interested. They are in this respect like good professors; they are intellectual pyromaniacs trying to kindle a spark of learning that will spread. Often they send professors notices of new books in their fields or of articles in current magazines. They are constantly distributing mimeographed lists of new accessions. Sometimes they even publish reviews intended to lure the reader to check out books about which they are enthusiastic.

If anything, the librarian may be a bit too eager in his attempt to have patrons read his books. Choosing books is like picking a wife; you like to make your own decision. Mother may favor a different mate for her son, but mother does not have to live with her choice. Sometimes in their eagerness librarians remind one of the old song of a very pathetic but genteel maiden, "Who'll buy, who'll buy, who'll buy my water cresses?" If this beating the drum for reading is a fault, it is on the side of generosity and certainly disproves the myth of the miserly librarian.[1] The modern librarian, then, is not happy when all his cataloged books are neatly arranged in the stacks. He is happy when his books are in use.

While the librarian is eager to lend the library's books, he expects to get them back at an agreed-upon time. He will be disturbed if a patron keeps a volume far beyond the date allowed and then grows insolent when reminded of his remissness. There are always a few who fancy themselves above the law, who feel that the rules were made for the other fellow. They want to know why there should be such a fuss over a few books.

Actually people seem to have no conscience about books. For that reason those who value their private collection do not keep books in open view at home. Friends look over shelves and say with a pleasant smile that cannot be denied, "I'm taking this book. O.K.?" You answer that it is O.K. but you know that there is a good chance that you will never see the volume again.

I am in sympathy with that courageous library director of East Orange, N.J., who in February, 1961, invoked a local ordinance and had police armed with warrants corral fourteen delinquent borrowers, some of whom had already retired for the night. Five of these could not furnish one hundred dollars bail and passed the night in a cell. As a result of this putsch, 1,500 books were returned and $450 in fines was collected. Admittedly this was drastic procedure. The public conscience in this matter should be awakened by a Return-the-Books-You-

Borrowed-Week. Television has declared May the Tavern Month; perhaps the bartenders will surrender just a week to the librarians.

Of course in a college there are enforceable penalties for not returning library materials. However, some who take books from a college library, especially where there are open stacks or browsing rooms, do not intend to return them. Librarians often complain of the numbers of books and magazines that are stolen. When this happens many hours are lost in searching for these books, and in reordering and cataloging them if they can be replaced. It is perhaps too much to ask teachers to deliver a lecture annually on the chain of losses occasioned by the theft of a single volume or magazine, but certain professors can at least prevent magazines from being cut up by not giving students the puerile task of making a notebook of clipped illustrations and articles on a given topic.

A second myth about librarians is that they worry over the bindings and the numbers on books and have no concern about their contents. What is often meant, it seems to me, is that librarians have no intellectual interests. One distinguished scholar recently wrote that the librarian reminds him of a headwaiter in a restaurant who leads diners to a table and places a menu before them. The simile is clever, but it is always dangerous to argue by parallels. The simile might be changed to the officer who sights an enemy through powerful glasses and then directs the firing of guns. The role of the librarian then receives a more favorable comparison. One wonders if the scholar who compares the librarian to a headwaiter is not confusing trained librarians with student assistants trusted with passing out books to patrons. These students are not considered librarians. Behind these clerks is a staff of specialists with advanced degrees. It is an example of ignorance in high places to say that these professional people are not interested in what is inside books.

Like other areas of graduate study, the library school strives to recruit the best. Some time ago I was asked by an assistant director of a library school to give my impressions of a certain student's intelligence, health, maturity, personality, and fitness for the library profession. This official indicated what his university expected of its candidates:

Success in the library field is largely dependent upon such qualifications as accuracy, good judgment, mental alertness, an interest in current progress in many lines, and a capacity for cooperation. Leadership in the profession requires initiative, executive ability, an attractive personality, as well as scholarship and experience. We hope to select only those candidates who are most promising, sparing other candidates the expense and discouragement of an unsuccessful experiment.

It is clear that this library school was recruiting only talent of the highest order. This letter was written in 1939. Twenty years later the theme of Alumni Day of the Columbia University School of Library Service was stated as "The Popular Image of the Library and the Librarian." In spite of the efforts of professors of librarianship and other leaders in the field, leading librarians felt that they had not been accorded the status they deserved. The discussion was summarized in this way:

From first to last, and in all the discussion, there was agreement that the road to recognition and status of the professional librarian, with an accompanying favorable image, is in the library's alliance with the other agencies of scholarship, the intellectual and artistic and cultural programs and persons in the institutions and communities the libraries serve.[2]

If the librarian feels that his stock has been a sluggish performer in the academic market place, he can blame in part the professor. He, too, is somewhat troubled about his status; he feels that he is not appreciated. Currently he regards the administrator as his natural enemy. He listens to official voices of the college explain that the administrator's justification for his existence is the aid he gives the teaching faculty; but the professor is inclined to question the claim of the administrators that they in practice act as the servants of the servants of the institution. He knows that these administrators learned about channels while serving as officers in the Second World War and that on their return to the halls of learning, they brought with them elaborate organizational procedures perfectly illustrating Parkinson's law. This smooth, well-oiled machinery functions in areas which the professor often regards as insignificant. The professor likes to explain that if teachers left the institution, there would be nothing left to administer. As a result he is at times bitter.

Whoever doubts this developing cleavage between top-heavy administrative forces and the teaching staff should spend a few hours leafing through the quarterly bulletin of the American Association of University Professors. Here will be found a list of institutions that have been censured after exhaustive investigation. Here the professor's importance and rights are stressed, and the conduct of harsh, illiberal, and unenlightened trustees and administrators is criticized without fear or mercy.

Now when an insecure professor finds that librarians wish to be treated as faculty members and not mere clerks, he may take the attitude that these, too, are a threat to the prestige of the professoriate. Not too well informed, he may accept a blurred image of the librarian. What he sees is a very unfair picture. Because the librarian does not engage in direct group instruction of students, it does not follow that his work is not important in the learning process. Certainly it is rash to conclude that he would not be able to expound in his area if put on the rostrum. The librarian cannot be expected to follow the intricacies of special problems in the more recondite fields of learning represented in the college catalogue; nor would the professor show any brilliance if he were taken out of his specialty. The librarian's knowledge may often be more broad than deep in many areas, but he, too, will have some special area of concentration in which he has considerable competence.

Librarians stand ready to perform a great many services of which faculty members are sometimes unaware. Professors who have done any research often have reason to thank a number of librarians for turning up some source material of which they were unaware or for running down obscure references written perhaps in a foreign tongue. How can a writer or a lecturer honestly underestimate the importance of those who help him with the material on which he may build or sustain his reputation? Teachers who object to treating librarians as faculty members may very well be those who rarely enter the library. They hardly live under the mandate: Publish or perish.

It is easy to believe that the librarian feels he is isolated. Actually he is not allotted the free time enjoyed by the teaching staff. A professor who is expected to do research often teaches nine hours a week, at the most twelve. However, in schools where research is not a *sine qua non* for survival, the number of hours is rarely set beyond sixteen. Such a schedule gives the professor plenty of time to drink coffee with his colleagues. A great deal of cross-fertilization between departments will naturally take place. This gives the professor a feeling that he belongs, that he has friends. But the librarian has no such light schedule. The work week for the librarian is often thirty-nine hours without coffee. His work is different from that of the professor; it is steady, unspectacular, routine in character, but always demanding. The teacher, after the intense concentration of fifty minutes—I am assuming that he is lecturing to the class and that he is not showing movies or having students make reports—may have reached an emotionally exhausting peak and must descend slowly to the lower levels with certain colleagues in a *Kaffeeklatsch* where he may still have enough energy to retain his title as the autocrat of the coffee break. But regulations do not permit the librarian such extended leisure. For this reason he may be on the fringe of campus socializing.

On the surface a great deal of honor is paid the library itself. It is called the treasury of learning, the home of the book—and nobody in the world, no matter how anti-intellectual, is hostile to *all* books. By an apt figure, the library is also called the heart of the college. From this heart life-giving volumes like corpuscles are constantly pumped throughout the academic community.

If the library is the heart of the college, just now it is suffering a great strain which it was never meant to bear. Librarians are on the point of becoming study hall custodians. Long before I read Mr. Lyle's confirming survey (see p. 73), a librarian pointed out to me that students in his college were using the reference and reserve rooms principally to read their class textbooks. This is not difficult to understand; the rooms are well-lighted and often air-conditioned. They furnish an excellent spot for cheap socializing.

Students claim that they cannot find in their rooms the quiet necessary for study. Married students are distracted by the wailing of the baby; fraternity houses and dormitories are noisy; in private homes the time wasters are always dropping in to chat. Instead of correcting the situation in which they live, students flee from the problem and so overcrowd the reading rooms that one who is genuinely interested in using the library for what it was intended, for consulting materials that may not be taken from the building, cannot find a place to sit. And when he does, he finds he must wedge himself in between pairs of softly cooing doves who claim to be studying together. A graduate student recently told me that the reading rooms at his university had become so noisy from undergraduate chatter that serious students were finding that the atmosphere was not conducive to concentration. We may eventually come full circle when we find that the library is too noisy for reading.

This is an area in which the college administration should try to understand the librarian's problem. If this type of service continues, libraries will have larger and larger reading rooms, but they will desert their real function. Actually the library in a large university cannot hope to solve the problem of furnishing a place where even a large percentage of the student body may study their class texts. In their desire to be of service, librarians may not choose to oppose this growth, but it is nevertheless an unhealthy growth. They should point out to administrators that there are other ways of solving this problem. To take on study hall chores would lead the profession down a dark bypath.

Sometimes librarians justifiably complain that certain areas of the library are taken over for functions that should be carried on elsewhere. One hears of libraries where registration day, that masterpiece of confusion in academic circles, is staged. If a student's first introduction to the library approaches bedlam, it will be difficult to convince him that the ideal on the following day is silence or at least a subdued voice. In order to court the benevolence of local organizations, college officials sometimes permit these groups to take over in an area normally intended for quiet, scholarly use. The librarian is not in a position to object too strenuously to administrators in these matters, but he knows that definite harm is done to the proper atmosphere that should prevail in the library.

Librarians are raising their voices in academic circles and are fast gaining recognition. Their publications are numerous, as a hasty glance under the heading LIBRARIES in the *Readers' Guide* will show. Through the American Library Association they have taken a liberal and often unpopular stand in the eyes of many citizens on the controversial issues of segregation, censorship of books, and the teacher's oath; in doing this they have lined up with the leading agencies of scholarship and culture.

Because of the nature of their work librarians may feel a bit isolated on college campuses, but only those who are unacquainted with their training and services will think of refusing them the rights and privileges of faculty members. Because their work serves every department in a college, librarians are the least expendable of all.

NOTES

1. A point which Hardin Craig also makes in "The Natural History of the Librarian." *AAUP Bulletin,* 46:399-405, December, 1960.

2. Robert D. Leigh and Kathryn W. Sewny, "The Popular Image of the Library and the Librarian." *Library Journal,* 85: 2089-91, June 1, 1960.

The
College Administration
and the Library

THIS TALK HAD its beginning in a joint meeting of college librarians and presidents at an institute on higher education. That is, it was supposed to have been a joint meeting, but the invitations to the institute were extended through the president's office and few seemed to have sifted down to the librarians. There was, however, a goodly sprinkling of deans and business managers in the audience. I had been asked to present the opening statement and took the opportunity to stress the need for a close relationship between administrative officers and librarians. I was followed by a university president who expressed in no uncertain terms his dissatisfaction with librarians in general and with what I had to say in particular. While I am happy to say that his opinion was by no means shared by all those in attendance, nevertheless I detected an undercurrent of dissatisfaction in some of the discussion which took place. Although I

Revised version of an address to the College and University Section of the North Carolina Library Association, Durham, N.C., October 27, 1961, originally published in *North Carolina Libraries*, 20:35-40, Winter, 1962.

am at a loss to say exactly what we could do to make dissatisfied presidents happier, I would suggest that at the next annual meeting of the North Carolina Library Association you invite college presidents to be present and that you get two or three presidents and librarians in a panel discussion, and let them get their troubles off their minds. My remarks today may perhaps serve as a basis for such a discussion.

That the effectiveness of the library is greatly hindered or enhanced by the relationship of the librarian to the president need hardly be mentioned. Libraries have to have books, and buildings to house the books. Librarians have to be selected, promoted, and paid. If, as one Texas president said about the faculty problems, these matters raise no eternal issues, they cannot be postponed and the eternal issues can.

If the relationship between librarians and administrators is not all that is to be desired,[1] we should frankly face up to the situation, discover the causes, and attempt to remedy them. I think there are three principal reasons for dissatisfaction:

The first is that the librarian has increasingly little opportunity to know the president personally. The president is a busy man. In recent years, an effort has been made to reorganize college administration so as to reduce the number of persons reporting to the president directly. The current trend seems to be to group all administrative functions under four high level officers who report to the president. These officers are the academic dean or vice-president on academic affairs, the director of student activities, the business manager, and the director of public relations. As a result of this type of reorganization, the librarian—long accustomed to going directly to the president to talk over his problems and to present his needs—now frequently finds himself reporting to the dean or vice-president. In saying this, I am saying simply that the librarian has less formal opportunity for conferences with the president than formerly and I am not for a moment trying to disparage the contribution which each of the other administrators can make to the library.

A second reason why library-administrative relations are not always what we would like them to be is simply that unshakable academic notion that librarianship is a technique and that librarians are technicians. Julian Boyd once put it bluntly and succinctly: "According to this view, held by too many presidents, . . . librarians are technicians, far below the rank of policy-makers. They are to keep the machinery going, to chart its mileage per gallon, to change its tires, and to keep it ready-fueled, but not to touch the steering wheel." [2] This is a view frequently held by faculty members. Without reference to its accuracy or fallaciousness, I think it explains why so frequently librarians are not taken into the councils of policy-makers and why administrators sometimes become understandably impatient of the amount of detail, not to mention the cost of the detail, involved in library work. I recall the remarks of a university president who said we probably needed to take a new look at the qualifications of librarians in the light of new developments in "information retrieval" and similar developments in technology applicable to libraries. Behind his statement was the implication that almost anyone could do the library job as well as, if not better than, the trained librarian provided specialists were brought in to set up and utilize automatic record and retrieval systems in library operations.

A third possible cause for disharmony in library-administrative relations follows logically from the other two. If the librarian has little opportunity to see the president and if in the opinion of the latter the librarian is primarily concerned with the mechanics of librarianship, it is not surprising that their approach to the solution of library problems is often widely divergent. This cleavage may be illustrated in both general and specific terms. In weighing a line of action on a particular request from a faculty member, let us say, the librarian considers the result of his decision on the quality of library service to others, the effect on present policies and procedures, and the extent to which the request will overtax the staff and library budget. The president's attitude toward a particular line of action is to "think of it in terms of its effect upon the reputation, the development, and the potential of the institution." [3] The man in the street may say there is no basis for conflict here but there is and it cannot be wished away. What the librarian thinks should be done in such matters as hours of opening, the acceptance of gifts, and loans to alumni and non-campus users is often widely divergent from what the president thinks and often insists should be done. Library policy, not necessarily mechanics or gadgets, is at the center of the librarian's consciousness. Is the granting of this or that request in line with library policy? If an affirmative decision will enhance the usefulness of the library to a particular professor and his class, can it be granted without sacrificing the interests of others who have a comparable claim upon library resources? If students want the library open longer hours for study hall purposes and beef up their demands by resolutions, petitions to the dean, and editorials in the student newspaper, the president may give them his support regardless of the effect on the quality of real library service. I quoted Dr. Harold Stoke briefly above. I am going to quote him again because his book, entitled *The American College President*, is one which every academic person can profitably read and ponder. Dr. Stoke writes that "the faculty," and here we might just as appropriately substitute the word "librarian," would like to have "all issues resolved on 'principle' as if the particular situation were detachable from everything else; the administration wants to settle nothing until its effect upon the fortunes and the future development of the institution can be assessed." [4]

Perhaps a more subtle situation involving differences in viewpoint will serve to illustrate what happens in dozens of instances and on dozens of campuses. The library of a university located in a large city does its best to assist non-campus users such as visiting scholars, industries, and local citizens who have need of research materials not available in the public library. It does not feel, however, that it can reach down its extra-curricular hand to assist school children. The librarian fears that library service

23

to the university's own students will suffer by the very effort to do too much. Moreover, he knows that school librarians are making a strong effort to build their own resources and that they are not likely to reach desirable standards if the school authorities feel they can always fall back on other local library resources. When a local teacher asked a desk attendant at the university library for permission for one of her brighter lads to use the library for a special project, the request was refused. The teacher was upset and spoke to a friend of the wife of the president who in turn placed the problem squarely in the lap of the president. The president was understandably upset by becoming involved in another problem. Moreover, he could see no earthly reason for withholding library privileges from this high school youngster, particularly in view of the fact that the university was anxious to attract bright students to its campus. His discussion with the librarian suggested a tendency on his part to regard all library users as equal in their claims for attention. Defensively, the librarian said he would take the matter up with the library committee. There was naturally a good bit of feeling on both sides. Admittedly it is not easy to strike the right balance between what is educationally desirable and what is administratively prudent but the example above illustrates the controlling and frequently different concerns of librarians and presidents.

What can be done to improve the administrative relationship to the library? Several things—of which I shall mention but three under these headings: definition of authority, communications, and staffing.

DEFINITION OF AUTHORITY

The unique, as well as the most obvious, thing the president can do to promote good administrative relations with the library is to define the librarian's authority and responsibility. The librarian does not need an *omnium gatherum* of laws but he does need a clarification of administration and faculty superstition and lore regarding the librarian's position. Is he responsible to the president directly or through the dean? Does the college library consist of all the collections of books in the possession of the college? Does the librarian have responsibility for the administration of library materials wherever they are located on the campus? Are phonograph records, music scores, educational film and other audio-visual aids to be regarded as library resources? What are the functions and duties of the library committee, what is the librarian's position on the committee, and how is rotation in office provided so that professors of English, mathematics, and physics can each in turn make their contribution to library progress? The absence of clearly defined policies on these and other matters will most certainly lead to a dispersion and weakening of library administrative strength, to departmental collections being sanctioned as *faits accomplis,* to restrictions on the use of library materials, and, above all, to loss of efficiency. I use the word "efficiency" not with the connotation of bustling activity but to signify one's ability to meet situations, to solve problems, whatever they may be. The successful librarian must work closely with administrators, deans, departmental chairmen, faculty, students, and others. Each of these has his own way of exerting pressure, his own special needs, and his own views on how the library should deal with all the varying groups on a college campus; hence the librarian will be most grateful to the college president who defines the major issues so that the librarian may assess his own position and plan a program of library development. A definite ruling in respect to the points outlined above should be expressed in legislation of the governing board. If this statement of issues is incorporated into the faculty handbook, or whatever other administrative device is used to inform the faculty, it will be of invaluable help to the librarian in rendering effective library service.

COMMUNICATIONS

Another important factor in library-administrative relations is communication. Indeed, the importance of adequate communication and personal acquaintance cannot be emphasized too strongly. The manifestations of the lack of communication are, in my opinion, innumerable and inescapable. New courses and curricular programs are introduced without special provision in the book budget to take care of the library materials needed to support them. New library buildings and new academic buildings with library quarters in them are planned without proper consultation with the librarian. Gifts are accepted by administrators without adequate space to house them, without funds to catalog them, and sometimes with commitments which are educationally unsound and which may prove to be a financial burden. One of the basic functions of administration is the facilitation of good communication. It becomes a travesty when what should be a real help to the library turns into a barrier.

How can the library keep itself from being physically and psychologically isolated from the college? There are both formal and informal channels of communication. The college president bears the chief burden of responsibility for opening up the formal channels. It is his responsibility to see that the librarian is represented, along with the chief administrative officers of the college, on the administrative council, the academic council if there is one, and the library committee. There are institutions where the librarian is not on any of these committees and the library administration is not in touch with the mainstream of administrative activity. One observes the symptoms as soon as one sets foot on the campus. Library support is meager, faculty interest in the library is dormant, and staff morale is low.

I do not think librarians can fight their way into the inner circle of administration by themselves. There seems to be a reasonable amount of evidence, however, that when the faculty speaks administrators hear and heed. The librarian's first tasks, therefore, are to identify the library with the faculty, library aims with teaching, and to transform latent faculty interest in the library into active resolve. As a first step in this direction the librarian needs to take a careful look at the library's way of doing things. The library is in one sense isolated from the faculty in that it is a separate unit of authority with the ever present danger that goes with independent units. Without being aware of it, the library may become disjoined from the faculty by day-to-day decisions at the operations level which crystallize into policies that are not understood or frequently misunderstood. Deficient in self-criticism, libraries and librarians can become almost pathologically sensitive to the criticism of others. Perhaps the best way to avoid isolation and to check narrowness in the interpretation of library policy is for the librarian to invite others to study library problems—administrators, the library committee, instructors, and students. Librarians must learn to be flexible and to consider suggestions with an open mind instead of immediately rejecting them. Former Librarian Goodrich of Dartmouth once offered librarians some invaluable advice: "Few things have more perplexed and annoyed me than the common habit of reacting against a scheme just because it is new. Since life and progress depend on change, it has seemed to me natural to consider new proposals with a friendly and open mind. When in doubt, try it. So many of my faculty colleagues have seemed to act as if their rule was 'when in doubt, do nothing.'" [5] Too many librarians have isolated themselves from the faculty by falling into the same error. If someone suggests opening the stacks they say the library was not designed for open stacks and the stack stairways are too narrow. If someone suggests opening a smoking room, they say the fire laws forbid it. This may be quite true, of course, but everyone on the campus knows the fire laws forbid smoking in classrooms and offices but no one pays any attention to them. If the library gets a reputation for letting faculty suggestions drop like a wet mop on the pavement, there is little likelihood that the president will see any real advantage in bringing the librarian into his advisory councils.

In the second place, I think it may be necessary in some colleges for the librarian to show why it is important for the library to be represented on administrative and faculty councils. Surely such representation is not important simply to give the librarian a listing in the college catalogue or merely as a status symbol. It is really not too important as a means of finding out what actions were taken on certain matters because sooner or later these things are reported through the grapevine or in the campus paper. The important point is that in taking part in these meetings the librarian hears the arguments pro and con, understands better the reasons why the particular decisions were reached, and learns something about the characteristic methods of operation and thinking of the administrators and faculty members who make the policies of the college. As a participant in discussion, he may not be voluble and he may not exert a great deal of influence but he can inform the administrators and faculty of the library implications of matters which come up for consideration.

These formal channels of communication are not the only means of keeping in touch with faculty and administrators. If anything, the librarian should make an even greater effort to know administrative officers and faculty personally. I have already mentioned negatively some examples of failure in library-administrative communications; let me now suggest positively several examples of the importance of personal acquaintance with the faculty. In the allocation of book funds, a knowledge of the nature of course programs and of individual faculty research is most helpful in reaching a fair proportioning of the funds. In selecting books, the librarian contributes most if, in addition to reading book reviews widely and critically, he knows something about the courses which professors offer. This is true in selecting books of a general nature as well as books which cut across departmental lines. The librarian should keep minutely posted on the current curriculum so as to have a sharp concept of the specific ways in which library support is possible and desirable. This problem of bringing faculty and librarians together, of inducing the faculty to consult with the librarians as well as the librarians with the faculty, and of developing a coherent unity in encouraging independent student use of the library, is not an easy task and not one which falls solely on the shoulders of the librarian and his staff. It is on this last point that all college librarians fervently wish that every faculty member would take to heart Dean Garland Taylor's admonition:

Whether you could or should allude to it, I also have a strong conviction that faculty members reduce library effectiveness in instruction by being themselves so ignorant of library resources and means of using them, by being lazy and indifferent with respect to their own potential utilization of books, and by wanting to thrust on the undergraduate library the burdens of research sources and services which are inappropriate to it.[6]

Dean Taylor's experience, unfortunately, is that of scores of college librarians.

Opportunity must also be sought for meeting administrators, faculty, and students as a group as well as individually. We are adept at helping individual readers in the library; we tend to shy away from group instruction. Consider, for example, the questions that really need to be answered in informing students about the use of study carrels in the stacks, which are, let us assume, restricted to the use of honors students. To understand the library's policy in assigning these carrels, the student needs to know about such matters as the purpose of the carrels, the demand for them in relation to the number available, the reason why there are restrictions on use, the importance of "charging materials" which are held in the carrels, and the rules of use. Rules can be posted in each carrel and regulations can be published in the library handbook. These tried methods are important, but how much better it would be if the head of the circulation department were to supplement them by arranging with the dean to talk with the honors students about carrel assignments at their first meeting of the year.

THE STAFF

The third factor I wish to mention in the improvement of library-administrative relations concerns the library staff itself.

Some mention has already been made of the contribution of the staff in the important matter of communications but the crucial position of the staff deserves a further word.

Even though the president is quick to recognize the importance of securing a first-rate person to head up the library, he is less likely to understand the need for an adequate staff. Yet one of the most serious weaknesses in college library administration today is understaffing and inefficient staffing. Adequate staffing is important in library-administrative relations for two reasons. The first is that the librarian must get the work done properly if the library is to be useful. The second is that the librarian must extricate himself sufficiently from detail to be able to plan the library's work, to keep in touch with administrators and faculty, and to gain some perspective on the aims of the college and on the library's part in fulfilling those aims. Relations with the administration begin to deteriorate when arrearages pile up, when library staffs are overtaxed, and when negative decisions become wearisomely monotonous.

As I have already stressed, the library needs a great deal of information to operate at a high level of effectiveness—information about course and special curricular programs, new buildings, accommodations outside the library for study, salary and wage prospects for students and clerical helpers on the campus, methods of purchasing and accounting, research interests of individual professors, photocopying facilities, and the like. Not all this information can be piped down through the person of the head librarian. Accordingly the staff has an important part to play in keeping the channels of communication open.

All this means is simply that each staff member has a responsibility for keeping the library informed so that it can be readily responsive to faculty and student needs. It does not imply that each staff member is expected to be equally at home in all the special situations which bring him into contact with administrative officers and faculty members, but rather that he should exercise whatever special talents he has to keep the library in touch with the mainstream of college activity. A staff member may be efficient in dealing with technical problems in the library yet his efforts may be futile in handling students. He may be a past-master in dealing with faculty on a personal basis and yet be ineffective in talking to a faculty group. The ideal, then, is the synthesis of all staff effort in forming close personal relationships with the administration, faculty, and students.

At the risk of creating a very unfavorable impression, I am going to mention briefly two other matters concerning the staff and library-administrative relations. The first is that I think it is important to have both men and women on the library staff and men in more nearly equal proportion to women. I think that more men on the staff, more manly men, that is, will help to improve library-administrative relations and will contribute also to staff morale. If you ask why I believe the presence of more men on the staff is important in this connection, I shall have to dodge the question by saying that I always espouse the cause of the underdog.

In the second place, I think it would help library-administrative relations if we librarians showed less concern than many of us do about matters of status.[7] I am for the head librarian seeking the highest salaries, a remuneration for librarians which makes librarianship as attractive financially as a career in college teaching, leaves of absence for scholarly study after a reasonable period of service, tenure, the right of a librarian to be appointed to a faculty committee in the same way that faculty members are afforded the opportunity to be appointed to library committees, and, of course, retirement and all the fringe benefits which normally apply to all university employees. I am all for the head librarian asserting the rights and privileges I have enumerated above and for the staff staying out of it. Library staffs which become deeply involved in problems of their own status tend to become obsessed with matters that are essentially personal. Librarianship is tyrannical enough without adding to it the strain of having to act like a professor. I feel that staff members should apply their time, energy, and initiative in ways which will earn

31

them status as a by-product. The challenge for librarians should always be to identify the library's opportunities for educational effectiveness and then to seek solutions instead of waiting for someone else to do so.

NOTES

1. "In fact I heard more derogatory language used among the eight presidents who made up the Commission on Financing Higher Education about librarians than I heard about any other component part of the university structure."—John D. Millet. *Quoted in:* Association of Research Libraries. *Minutes,* January 31, 1954, Madison, Wis., Appendix VI; "The college or university librarian today is rarely the object of his master's affection."— Reuben Frodin. *In:* H. H. Fussler, ed., *The Function of the Library in the Modern College.* Chicago, University of Chicago Graduate Library School, 1954, p. 100.

2. Julian Boyd, "The Librarian Reports to the President." Southern University Conference. *Proceedings . . .* 1950. Birmingham, April 11-12, 1950, p. 106.

3. Harold W. Stoke, *The American College President.* N.Y., Harper, 1959, p. 153.

4. *Ibid.*

5. Nathaniel L. Goodrich, "A Fairy Tale." Dartmouth College *Library Bulletin,* 4:75, February, 1945.

6. Garland Taylor, letter to the author, June 24, 1960.

7. Administrators concerned with problems of staff status for librarians in their colleges will find a useful summary of practice in Robert B. Downs, ed., *The Status of American College and University Librarians* (ACRL Monograph No. 22, Chicago, A.L.A., 1958). An analysis of standards of the large regional accrediting associations reveals that all except the Northwest Association specify faculty status for the head librarian while the Southern Association provides that all members of the professional staff shall be given faculty status and rank; the

Western College Association extends faculty status to the professional heads of departments as well as to the chief librarian.—Fritz Veit, "The Status of the Librarian According to Accrediting Standards of Regional and Professional Associations." *College and Research Libraries*, 21:127-35, March, 1960.

Developing the College Library Book Collection

THERE IS a cocklebur tenacity about certain minor phrases that refuse to be shaken out of the language. On a par with the "future lies ahead" and "roll back the cost of living" are "the library is the heart of the college" and "a college library is as good as the faculty it serves." These library maxims are trite but they serve a useful purpose. They identify the central importance of (1) the library in the college educational program, and (2) the faculty's role in the selection of books for the library. In theory they are soothing; in practice they are more than likely to prove disappointing. Anyone who has visited widely among colleges in this country, particularly among smaller colleges, can only conclude that most of their libraries are half-starved and that their collections, like Topsy, "just growed"—instead of developing according to plan. Here and there one may find beautiful exceptions but in most cases there is room for a great deal of improvement in the selection of books for the college library.

An address to the College Libraries Section of the Association of College and Research Libraries, Miami, Florida, June 20, 1962.

I start from the premise that you cannot have a first-rate library without a systematic, resourceful, and enlightened program of book acquisition. This is not a simple task, nor, probably, is there a definitive course of action which will fit all college situations. There are, however, some things which should be avoided and some few principles which should be recognized. We may start by considering four negative aspects of the problem.

First, it may be tediously repetitive to point out that size has no meaning as a goal in building a college library; but it cannot be said too often. That one college has ten thousand more library books than another is no sign of academic health. A college library of ten thousand volumes which discards one thousand at the end of the year may be a far better library than one with thirty thousand volumes and no discards. Everyone agrees with this in principle but all too many are humbugged into striving for size in practice. Why is this so? No sane librarian really wants to increase his book stock merely to amass an impressive comparative total. The simple truth of the matter is that a large volume count, whether in total holdings or annual additions, is regarded as a mark of distinction in the academic world and college presidents and faculty members take pride in a rapidly growing library. There is a second reason for the emphasis on quantitative assessment. It is much simpler to count the number of volumes in a book collection than to make a qualitative appraisal of it.

As long as size is considered a symbol of library strength, the effort to develop a fine, selective library will be handicapped. There is no reason, of course, why librarians of high intention should submit to the operation of Parkinson's law. They can, if they wish, eliminate the count of total volumes from their published tables of comparative statistics. The regional accrediting associations no longer suggest that a library should have a certain number of volumes in order to be respectable. Indeed, their executive secretaries and visiting teams play down the importance of size in the library and encourage colleges to weed their collections. In spite of this, there will always be administrators and faculty members who will ask: how do we know when we have reached adequacy in our library? How many volumes should we have in this field or subject? The reply here is the answer William Warner Bishop gave some thirty years ago. He said, "Enough!" Enough of the basic scholarly periodical literature, with strong back files, in the various disciplines. Enough of the basic source material in the form of government documents, manuscripts, and first editions. Enough of the classics, reference books, standard works, and general run of books of first importance in all fields of the curriculum. Enough of the current output of new fiction, travel, biography, poetry, drama, and other books, which appears to be of primary worth and which has faculty and undergraduate though not necessarily curricular interest. Well, having heard this answer, there still will be those who rise to ask: "But what do you mean by enough or how are we to know when we have enough?" The answer to these questions necessarily leads to specifics. If the question relates to the category of new fiction, drama, or poetry, one answer might be: "Take a careful look at your shelves. If you do not have at least eighty per cent of the following writers represented, not in a single title but by their best work, then you do not have enough": Bertolt Brecht, William Styron, C. P. Snow, Christopher Fry, Anthony Powell, J. D. Salinger, Graham Greene, Vladimir Nabokov, Morley Callaghan, François Mauriac, Santha Rama Rau, Richard Hughes, Ignazio Silone, H. E. Bates, Saul Bellow, John Osborne, Angus Wilson, Iris Murdoch, Honor Tracy, Ivy Compton-Burnett, James Gould Cozzens, Bernard Malamud, James Baldwin, Richard Wilbur, Alberto Moravia, James Michener, John O'Hara, Tennessee Williams, Evelyn Waugh, Kingsley Amis, Arthur Miller, Eugène Ionesco, William Golding, Lawrence Durrell, Carson McCullers, Gore Vidal, Eudora Welty, and V. S. Pritchett.

A second fact to bear in mind is that the building of a first-rate college library is not the product of overnight buying. New colleges are springing up everywhere across the land; the young are knocking ever more loudly at the college door. The attitude of the leaders in higher education and the public at large appears to be "let all come who desire to come"—if necessary by establishing junior colleges, doubling the size of classes, adding dormitories, or teaching in temporary buildings. Everyone agrees that the most crucial problem is faculty—and surely it is—but what is even more striking and perhaps even a little sinister is the lack of concern about libraries on the part of any but a few of the most enlightened and responsible leaders. Without a good library, there can be no college.

A colleague in noting this symptom of the times has referred to the new institution as the "library-less" college. What actually happens in practice, one gathers, is that the realization of the library need comes somewhat confusedly and somewhat late. Here is a letter from the library clerk of one of these Johnny-come-latelies who would like to slip his eggs into our nest for us to hatch:

Dear Sirs:

We are soon to become a liberal arts college, and in anticipation of this achievement we would like to build up a library that would sufficiently meet the needs of a liberal arts college.

Would you perhaps have a list of suggested books for a liberal arts college? If so, we would appreciate your cooperation in sending us such a list. If there is not a list already compiled, it would be extremely helpful to us if you would make up a short list that you feel would be adequate. . . .

Sincerely,

Library Assistant

Even among respected colleges, the deliberation which once characterized earlier curricular planning is now giving way to an impatience which seeks to multiply courses without proper concern for the supporting library materials. As a consequence, almost every library survey one reads points to the need for a large "make-up" or "overtake" fund to fill in gaps and eliminate arrearages. The promised land cannot be reached this way. Good libraries are the result of careful day-by-day selection in response to the expressed needs of departments; not of a hasty and impatient stampede to make up for lost time. Good libraries come only by a slow process of growth and development. Growth inevitably requires the expenditure of ever-increasing sums of money; but to achieve development there must also be wise selection and a careful use of available resources.

A third point to be emphasized is that good collections are not developed by an excessive dependence upon recommended book lists. There is no substitute for a thorough acquaintance with books through the reading of critical reviews and the books themselves. The recommended lists of individual libraries or associations have their value. They may encourage the librarian to take an active lead in book selection and they are helpful in appraising the quality of a collection in a particular field or fields; they cannot replace rigorous and systematic staff-faculty effort to select books in fields in which they are thoroughly grounded. Constant dependence upon booklists transforms the librarian into an administrative clerk. The warning voiced by Professor John W. Spargo of Northwestern University, several years ago, merits repeating here. Speaking to reference librarians, he charged:

At this point I must pause to cast an unmannerly slur upon those reference librarians who merely check over mechanically this, that, or the other list of reference books when establishing or augmenting a collection. This is one way to do it, of course, and I suspect that it is the way most often employed. The case is that, when you simply check a list mechanically against the holdings of your reference collection, you are turning yourself into that monument of folly, the scholar away from his books.[1]

Recommended lists are suggestive, stimulating, and, when properly used, a helpful aid to selection. They should be used for reference and study, not, as Spargo makes abundantly clear, for mechanical checking and subsequent book purchasing. There is no nourishment in checking and ordering from a recommended booklist, but to read reviews critically and then to check one's final estimate against a scholarly appraisal in something equivalent to that valuable bibliographical casualty, *The United States Quarterly Book Review* (1945-1956), is quite another thing.

A fourth principle is that no single individual should be allowed to exercise undue control over the activities connected with building the library collections. Whenever a department head or individual professor dominates the selection and acquisition process, there is inevitably a disinclination on the part of other faculty members to participate fully. An authoritative attitude toward selection, sometimes mistakenly interpreted by librarians as an indication of "library-mindedness" on the part of a professor, chokes off, in their early stages, those younger members of the faculty who could give their time and interest to the library. They cannot be blamed when their efforts in this direction are frowned upon by a department head. Individual professors, however, are no more prone to exaggerate their own importance in library development than librarians. The librarian has a job of leadership but he should use his office to coordinate and inform and not to dominate book selection. If occasionally he becomes impatient with what appear to be the procrastinating and slipshod selection methods of his teaching colleagues, he should not compound their faults by taking over their selection responsibilities. The librarian who assumes a proprietary right over library book funds and selection procedures inevitably represses the motivation which he is supposed to foster.

This is perhaps enough of the negative. For a more positive approach to the development of an imaginative program of building book collections, it is obvious that there must be a "working combination" of administrators, faculty, and library staff. Each has his role to play and the librarian cannot delegate his part. Despite his preoccupation with budgets, building, and staffing, the college librarian must make the development of the book collections his major concern. It is a task in which he should receive help from the faculty and the members of the administration and library staff but for which he must assume the ultimate responsibility, and he must know how to set about it.

To promote this "working combination," there are certain components which a college will be compelled to incorporate into its library program. Among these are: (1) a clear understanding of what kind of library the college is supposed to be building and for what kinds of users; (2) a genuine and general awareness of "the different roles which different books . . . play in the intellectual life of those who come to . . . [the] library";[2] (3) an effective organization for involving the faculty and library staff in book selection; and (4) a liberal and assured annual fund with regular annual increases for book purchases. Each of these concepts deserves brief examination.

LIBRARY GOALS

Statements of educational goals are not too much help to the library. Aims are defined and redefined from time to time by trustees and presidents—with, it is hoped, faculty consultation— but these are likely to be so general as to be of little worth to the library. The aim may be to produce community leaders, to develop the student's critical ability, to train young people for useful occupations, or to prepare students for graduate work and the professions. All these are interesting and worth-while goals but they do not furnish a guide to measuring the book needs of the library. What the librarian needs to know is something down to earth, something which he can only obtain from the president or faculty or both. Is the student body to be restricted in number or are fairly substantial enrollment increases anticipated? The answer has a bearing on library study and reading space accommodations and the staffing of the circulation services. Is the aim of the college to be a four-year liberal arts college or a miniature university? A library properly subordinate to a liberal arts college is bound to a policy of high selectivity in building collections. If curricular offerings are to be multiplied or if master's offerings are contemplated, this calls for quite a different sort of library. When master's courses are introduced in certain fields, and if other departments in the college are then expected to serve a supporting role in master's degree-granting programs, there is bound to be an increasing emphasis on research even though the courses were not originally structured as research oriented. As a result the library will be required to include among other resources many more specialized journals and bibliographical tools. The cost of library growth will rise sharply. Is there likely to be an emphasis on independent study and honors work? For those who take for granted that the library will be able to take care of these needs, here is contrary evidence from an experienced librarian: "The writer can cite from his own college the necessity for obtaining *Monatshefte für Mathematik und Physik* for an honors in mathematics, the use of our file of a London newspaper published during the Napoleonic era by a preseminar student studying British public opinion on the War of 1812, and the need of buying photocopies of contemporary French documents for a course on the French Revolution. . . ."[3] If the college is denominational, in what way do the distinctive concerns of this type of college affect the content of the library's collections? If the college is somewhat isolated from larger library resources, does the college expect the library to support individual research and study for advanced degrees by faculty members from purchase as well as loans? If so, the administration will need to provide additional book funds for this purpose as well as subsidize loans and photocopies. Does the curriculum provide for a basic program of liberal education for all undergraduates or does it permit specialization early in the student's career? In the first instance, provision will have to be made for appropriate reading materials and library accommodation. Such questions should be answered in the light of deliberate policy and not as the by-product of circumstance and pressure. The library will be able to control and plan its growth far more usefully if the librarian knows the goals and outcomes contemplated by the president.

The second component of successful book collection building is the recognition by the administration and faculty that it takes different types of books to fill different needs in curriculum support and that each of these needs requires a rational and systematic program of book selection and book buying. There are, for example, *reference* books which are needed for answering reference questions, for supplying background information, and for literature search. Everyone takes for granted that the college library must have a good reference collection, but few colleges make proper provision for its establishment and maintenance. Reference books are costly and provision must be made for an assured annual allocation to buy them and also for a librarian of sound judgment, deep learning, and wide experience to select them. A second group of books which contributes to a good college library collection comprises the so-called *standard* works, books which everyone recognizes as being outstanding, as well as current works in each subject field of the curriculum. The judgment and knowledge for the selection of the latter must come from the subject specialists on the faculty. An effective organization is almost as important here as book knowledge but of this I shall speak later. Suffice it to say now that the *standard* works form the heart of the library collection. They must be there in each field, in the best complete editions, and with the best critical commentaries. A third type of book needed in college work is usually described as the *general* book and by this is meant the book which bridges the gaps between the subjects taught or which is of a general nature and intended for the educated reader. The librarian and his staff are chiefly responsible for these books and here, as in the selection of *standard* works in the special fields, it is essential to read widely and to have a continuing and systematic plan for making the proper selections. A final group of books may be described as *special collections—* rare books, manuscripts, maps, college archives, and some primary research material. Do such materials have a place in the college library? The answer is undoubtedly yes, and an example may help to illustrate their usefulness. A student wishes to know what views a person in the seventeenth century held to cause him to be called an atheist by his contemporaries. Not satisfied with a seventeenth century dictionary definition of atheism he consults the card catalog under the seventeenth century philosopher "Descartes" and finds a reference to Henry More's *A Collection of Several Philosophical Writings*, published in London in 1672. The fact that More, a fellow of Christ's College, Cambridge, belonged to a group of Christian Platonists and was strongly attached to the Church of England renders his opinion on the subject of atheism important. The student found this book in the college library's rare book collection, studied it, and discovered that More did not consider Descartes an atheist, but that he did consider other men atheists. By comparing the views of these other men with those of Descartes, the student was satisfied that he could answer the question.

These four types of materials—reference books, standard works, general books, and special collections—are not the only types which make up the college library book collection but they are the most important ones. To the extent that their distinctive nature, purpose, and necessary provision are not recognized because of the indifference of administrators and faculty or the incompetence of the librarian, to that extent the college library will prove to be something less of a library than it might or should be.

AN EFFECTIVE ORGANIZATION

A third element in building the library collection which it is important for administrators and faculty members to take into account is the need for an effective organization. In the academic world, to be sure, the idea of organizing anything is likely to be anathema to many; yet without it the selection of books for the college library is haphazard and incomplete, and in many cases, even with the best of instructors, likely to be superficial. Good library collections are the product of a coherent plan of acquisitions and unflagging assiduity. One may buy books for one's own private library without too much contrivance but this method certainly does not suffice for a college which is spending thousands of dollars each year on books for its library. By organization is meant nothing more than that the library and faculty should have formulated procedures for selecting and acquiring books which will serve to give the whole task a sense of direction and which will have definite use every day as a guide to ordering. Organization, moreover, means more than a plan or device for doing things. It also implies that the administrator, faculty member, and librarian recognize the importance of book selection in the educational process and encourage widespread participation in doing a quality job. It is primarily upon the president that the responsibility falls for securing adequate book funds. He makes it possible for the librarian, the faculty, and the library staff to do their part. Each of these parts deserves brief mention.

The Librarian's Part

In this organization, the librarian is concerned with the book development program as a whole as well as with his specific responsibilities in selection. He will see that policies and procedures for selecting and recommending each of the various types of books—reference works, standard works, general books, and special collections—are clearly formulated and made known to the faculty. He will arrange for faculty-library representatives in each department or division to channel orders to the library and to receive recommendations, dealers' catalogs, and book notes from the library. He will allocate the book fund with the advice of the library committee, making proper provision for funds to acquire each of the groups of books which make up the college collection. He will do everything possible to ensure that there is a two-way flow of information and ideas from the library to the newest instructor on the faculty and from the junior staff member to the librarian. Because of his pivotal place in the book selection program, he will have the final responsibility for book purchasing and this will include the right to approve or disapprove book orders which seem grossly out of line with library policy.

The Faculty's Part

The faculty has a twofold responsibility in building up library resources in subject fields. The first is to keep the collection up to date by a careful selection of new publications and a weeding of the old. The second is to fill gaps in the collection.

Nobody has ever devised a perfect method for doing either of these jobs. Each teaching department has its own method, and each plan has its own merits. Two elements, however, characterize the best of these plans: (1) a systematic approach, by which all areas of the field are covered, and (2) a division of responsibility, whereby all members of the department participate in the selection program. First, there should be a systematic survey of present library holdings in the field. This could be done by checking the library catalog against certain standard lists and selected titles compiled by the faculty from the book review sections of the scholarly journals. Each instructor would be made responsible for surveying needs in the field of his special interest. He would be instructed to list all books that he thinks a good college library should have. Such a checking would probably result, depending upon the strength of the collection, in a list of several hundred titles not in the library which the faculty of the department deem desirable for purchase. Since it is unlikely that funds would be available for purchasing all of the backlog of books, the faculty would then be asked to break the list down into three parts: (1) essential books, urgently needed; (2) books vitally needed, but for which the need is not immediately pressing; and (3) books needed but not vitally or urgently.

The problem of *current* selection requires the allocation of responsibility to each member of the department for checking systematically the reviews in scholarly journals in his respective

45

subject in order to keep the collection up to date. Each person in the department will have to read reviews regularly when the journals are "checked in," and suggest titles in his particular field. Faculty members as well as librarians will discover that reading reviews can become a habit, one that can be cultivated and enjoyed, but one which must be pursued systematically. If the faculty member or librarian falters in his regular study of current reviews, his contribution to building a fine, selective library is impaired.

There are no doubt other ways to organize faculty participation in book selection. If they provide a systematic approach and a division of responsibility, given one condition, they will prove equally good. The one condition is that there shall be a department-library representative in each department who is sufficiently capable, conscientious, and perceptive to see that the departmental plan is carried out. In this naughty world of competition a spirit of dedication is perhaps too much to expect. Librarians should campaign strongly for recognition of the department-library representative's task. His teaching load should be reduced substantially during his two- or three-year period of service. If this is not possible, he should be released from all other committee work.

The Library Staff's Part

In leaving to the last an account of the library staff's part in developing the library collection, it is not the intention to detract from its contribution. Indeed, it is physically impossible for the head librarian to do all that he might do and in consequence he must depend on certain members of the library staff to assist in the selection of general and reference books. All staff members aid in building a good college library but not all in the same way. The diversity of possible activities is great indeed and it is folly to think that all librarians have the same abilities. Some have managerial qualities and are superb in organizing library services to readers. Some have technical and scholarly aptitude for cataloging and classifying books. Others add luster to the library's position in the college by the excellence of the reference assistance given to individual readers. But only a few who read widely and critically have the ability, tenacity, and opportunity to apply their talents to the building of a fine college library collection. What most colleges lack is a realization of the need for first-rate librarian-bookmen on its library staff and a willingness to pay for these qualities. What most college librarians overlook when they have such people on the staff is the need for giving them plenty of time to read book reviews and discuss with one another the significant books which they think should be added to the library. More vision is essential on the part of college administrators in financing library appointments and on the part of college librarians in recognizing conspicuous book selection ability and encouraging those so qualified to spend more of their time on this important task.

The library staff's contribution to developing the library collection is made chiefly in the realm of general and reference books. In the university library, there is nothing novel about assigning the choice of reference books to the reference librarian and allocating money for this purpose, but it is unfortunate that in the college, which needs them most, there are too few reference librarians and still fewer who are qualified to select reference books. In the choice of general books there are the obvious titles which require no particular skill in selection and which most college libraries will buy almost automatically even though the acquisition of any book without reading at least one critical review is perhaps questionable. The point where real discrimination is needed is the selection of those titles which the library *might* be expected to buy and those still more difficult-to-decide-on titles which classify as *would-be-nice-to-have*. It is in the selection of these materials—general histories and histories of literature as well as imaginative literature not covered in curriculum courses, social history, books which cover a specific subject but which are general in treatment, biography and autobiography, travel, general science, and particularly contemporary literature—that the library staff can supplement and extend the selections of the subject specialists on the faculty. When exciting new works of imaginative literature appear, students should have an opportunity to read them. The professor has many concerns in library matters but the selection of contemporary novels, poetry, drama, and essays is not one of them.

Book reviews are not the only basis of evaluation. The need or potential need of the title must be taken into account. The extent to which a particular book supplements, complements, or extends knowledge beyond other books on the same subject already in the library is another important factor. And because many librarians come into their profession through a major in English or social science, it is all the more important that books in science should not be neglected. Selections by the methods I have suggested can come *only* from wide experience in reading reviews and in reading books. If one reads reviews of books he has read and knows well, he can form, over a period of time, bases for evaluating reviews and reviewers.

AN ADEQUATE ANNUAL BOOK FUND

The fourth element in building the college library book collection is money. All libraries are alike in that they contain books, and all are alike in that their librarians never have sufficient funds to buy all the books that are needed. Smith College, for example, spent $70,000 for books and journals in 1960-1961; Davidson, an equally fine but smaller college, spent $17,000; but in neither case was the amount large enough to satisfy the demands for books made upon the libraries. Many factors affect the probable expenditure of book funds such as the teaching methods in the college, price inflation in the book world, or arrears in existing collections, but in the last analysis the amount each college library needs for book purchases is largely determined by the bibliographical zeal of its faculty. A college faculty which is content with limited book funds will in all probability reflect a long-time conditioning to poverty or a predominantly class-textbook method of teaching.

Unfortunately book demands cannot be too accurately forecast in the early months of the year when budgets have to be prepared. Consequently, the librarian is advised to undertake a continuous survey of book needs with the faculty which will enable him to budget more accurately than, let us say, on the basis of the past year's book fund. Some guidance, however, is afforded by a comparison of the budget estimate with the book and periodical expenditures of other college libraries. The average book and periodical expenditure of 279 member colleges of the Association of American Colleges from which data for 1960-1961 are available was $12,396.[4]

Through the experience of librarians, the Association of College and Research Libraries has established that it takes a minimum of five per cent of the general and educational expenditures of a college adequately to support a strong library.[5] The Association's standards suggest that out of the total amount for library purposes it will be necessary to spend at least one dollar for books for every two dollars for staff and operation. This ratio may vary somewhat from library to library, but it is interesting to note that according to the latest figures the best college libraries spend approximately in this ratio without having planned consciously with this end in view. The necessity of providing more liberally for library support and of spending carefully the funds the library receives for books is accentuated by the inflationary spiral of the past two decades.[6]

Here then are four principles which, in my opinion, are necessary for success in developing a fine college library book collection. To repeat, these principles are: a crystal-clear understanding of what kind of library the college is supposed to be building, a genuine and general awareness of the different types of books which are needed to fill various uses in the curriculum support, an effective organization for involving the faculty and library staff in book selection, and sufficient funds to ensure adequate coverage through wise selection of the current output of books and journals. There are, of course, other elements, but if the college president, professor, and librarian have a firm grasp of their views on and solutions to the problems raised by these four principles, plus an understanding of the negative aspects of book selection stated at the beginning, then the library will in time be able to boast an outstanding collection and a systematic, enlightened, and imaginative program of developing the collection.

NOTES

1. John W. Spargo, "Book selection for reference work." *In:* Pierce Butler, *The Reference Function of the Library.* Chicago, University of Chicago Press, 1943, p. 268.

2. John A. Lester, "The Library's Role in a Liberal Education." *Library Journal,* 85:491, February 1, 1960.

3. Carrol H. Quenzel, "The College Library—an Intellectual Catalytic Agent." University Center in Virginia. *News Bulletin,* 2:1, May, 1962.

4. *Library Statistics of Colleges and Universities, 1960-61, Institutional Data,* by John C. Rather and D. C. Holladay. Washington, D.C., U.S. Office of Education, 1962 (OE-15023-61). The data included only colleges whose enrollments were between 500 and 1500 and excluded liberal arts colleges of universities.

5. "Standards for College Libraries." *College and Research Libraries,* 20:274-80, July, 1959 (reprinted in the Appendix of this book, p. 76-86).

6. *The Cost of Library Materials: Price Trends of Publications,* by Frank L. Schick and William H. Kurth. Washington, D.C., U.S. Office of Education, 1961 (OE-15029A).

Use and Misuse
of the
College Library

WHY DO STUDENTS come to the library? The average librarian, asked this question, would probably say that students come to the library to write term papers, to find the answers to specific questions, and to read reserve books. I might have added, depending of course on the person with whom I was talking, that a few students come looking for a date, to pass the time away, to pick up a book or journal for recreational reading, or occasionally, perhaps, to study. Now, however, I would not be so naïve, for I have been making an informal investigation of the library habits of college students and I find that they are much more circumscribed. Indeed, I suspect the results of a similar survey in your own libraries will provide a wholesome shock to any of you who, like President Henry M. Wriston, have been waging war on "assignments" in favor of "independent study." [1]

The statistics of library use regularly kept and reported by libraries have their value but they do not tell the whole story

An address to the College Section of the Georgia Library Association, Jekyll Island, Georgia, October 26, 1961.

and in some respects they may even be misleading. By ignoring the use of books and other library materials *inside* the library, they leave out what amounts to a substantial part of the use of most college and university libraries. Moreover, statistics of home use are purely quantitative; they do not even provide a clue to the kinds of users and types of materials used. Of course, the reason why libraries have omitted *inside* library use from library statistics is simply that it is not feasible to make a complete count of all the books used. To keep such detailed records regularly would require more staff than the results could possibly justify. But while it is impossible to record all library use continuously, it is possible to keep detailed figures for a short time. A "spot census," covering even as brief a period as one day, provides a statistical basis for generalizing about total library use that is lacking in existing statistics. Such a census can throw light on the reasons why students come to the library and the number who come and from what classes. It can tell something, though not with complete accuracy, about the number of publications used within the library. And it can dispel our ignorance regarding the kinds and variety of materials which students use when they come to the library.

With such a purpose in mind and with a view to gathering some necessary background information on the question as to how students may be motivated to use the library for independent study, I asked fifteen college and university librarians to make a one-day study of student library use in the month of April, 1961. For this purpose I suggested using a one-page questionnaire (Appendix, p. 73) which would be handed out to students as they entered the library and picked up as they left the building. I am well aware of the limitations of the questionnaire. It is an imperfect communication, the responses often being like one of those picture postcards sent home by holidaymakers with the words "Having a wonderful time, X marks my room." In this case there was the additional disadvantage that some students, in a hurry, may have filled it out with even less sincerity and care than is customarily accorded a holiday postcard. Moreover, the data turned up are quantitative and afford only a partial picture. No one in his right mind, either, would claim that a one-day study is necessarily typical of the use of the library on other days. Nevertheless, I believe that a more comprehensive and carefully controlled study of library use would not alter materially the primary conclusions which I have drawn from this limited study.

The one-day study confirms what all of us have long taken for granted, namely, that the outside or home use of library materials is only a part of library use. It shows that for every book taken outside the library for home use, and this includes overnight reserve books, there are four library items used within the building. To be quite fair, one must add that the materials taken out of the library are usually books; the materials used within the library embrace the total library resources and may include a book, a record, a document, a periodical, or a newspaper.

Who uses the library? Here the conclusions are less interesting because more obvious than the reasons given for coming to the library. Approximately 8,500 students used the libraries, some more than once during the day the check was made. This figures out to one user to every three students enrolled in the colleges. Freshmen were the heaviest users, followed by sophomores, juniors, and seniors—in that order. In proportion to their enrollment, however, more juniors and seniors used the library than freshmen and sophomores. Several librarians were surprised by the number of students who were repeaters during the one-day study. In one library, for example, approximately a third of the questionnaires returned came from students who had used the library more than once during the day. "I'm astonished at the number of times some people enter the library," writes one librarian, "some of them," he added, "to use the lavatories."

More revealing than who uses the library are the reasons given by students for coming to the library. Their replies are often astonishing and upset many an oft-held idea. For example, it has been generally thought by librarians that general education and changing methods of instruction during the past decade have resulted in a greater use of total library resources and a consequent breaking away from large dependence upon textbook and assigned readings. When I questioned twenty-nine college librarians about this matter a year or two ago, eighteen said that they *thought* the trend was toward greater independent library use and less textbook use. The results of the one-day test show without a shadow of a doubt, however, that a large majority of those who enter the library go there to study their own textbooks. The respondents to the questionnaires check this reason three times more frequently than any other. A majority of those who use the library are not working *with* library materials; they are working *beside* library materials. Approximately the same number come to look up material for a research paper as come for reserve reading and for "charging out," returning, and renewing books. When the number of different types of publications used within the library is analyzed, however, reserve books are mentioned more frequently than reference books and current periodicals.

A fairly large number of students gave reasons other than assigned reading, term papers, and the return of books for coming to the library. Slightly more than 6 per cent come for general reading unrelated to class assignment. It would be interesting to know what they read. A larger number checked "other reasons" and this group is an interesting one. Aside from such facetious replies as "to get out of the rain" or "to buy a piece of tutti-frutti gum," a large number said they came to listen to records, to write letters, and to "meet someone." A few gave reasons which sounded as though they might be trying to impress the world with their reading stamina but a larger number were obviously very honest—among them the ones who said they came "to pick up their notebooks," to look at "good-looking women" and "to sleep."

The number of books, journals, and other library materials which students said they read in the library varied from one to

54

three items per student. Students were asked to total the number of items used under such headings as reference books, reserve books, current periodicals, microtext, phonograph records, current newspapers, pamphlets, and other books and journals. This last category was intended to cover books and bound journals not accounted for under reference and reserve books. Of the total number of items consulted or read, 30 per cent belonged in the "other books and journals" category, 17 per cent were reference books, 19 per cent were reserve books, 18 per cent were current periodicals, and 8 per cent were newspapers. These findings coincide to some extent with our normal conceptions of library use although I was surprised to learn that current periodicals are used as extensively as they are. This would appear to make the role of periodicals all the more important in college education, although I am not sure that these quantitative figures mean anything more than that students are reading what is fed them by Henry Luce.

Let me try to put together, as simply and as briefly as I can, the results of this study:

First, more than 50 per cent of all students using the libraries were using their own textbooks exclusively; 16 per cent were using library materials for independent study.

Second, one student in three came to the library; juniors and seniors were the heaviest users in proportion to their numbers.

Third, the number of publications used inside the library was four times greater than the number of books charged out for home use.

This pattern of student use of the library carries with it certain implications for college administrators and teachers. I shall conclude by suggesting the nature of these implications:

(1) It is clear that no matter what administrators or librarians say or do about it, many students will continue to use the library as a study hall. If the library is the only study hall on the campus, it will not accommodate those who wish to study without overcrowding the reference, reserve, browsing, or other

special reading rooms of the library and interfering with readers who want to use these rooms and the library books housed there for the purposes for which they were intended. Provision for study outside the library and dormitories is an absolute necessity if the library is to be an important factor in improving college instruction.

(2) On the assumption that many students will come to the library to study their texts, study halls should be provided for this purpose.[2] In planning a new library building, one or more study halls should be provided in the library and should be so arranged that they can be reached by a separate outside entrance after the library is closed.

(3) The faculty have the primary responsibility for structuring the academic courses for independent study. Present teaching practices would appear to provide little incentive for students to do substantial and rewarding reading. If professors are wedded to the idea of using textbooks and reserve readings, there is little the librarian can do about making changes. He should, however, continue to exert his influence in working with individual professors to promote independent library use and to this end he should create a library atmosphere conducive to tutorial instruction. For example, he should encourage the discussion of books by providing talking rooms near to reading rooms, make available as many private studies as possible in place of large reading tables, and provide for the most effective display of materials such as government publication sources, maps, manuscripts, and the like. Finally, as a first step in calling attention to the over-dependence of students upon textbook reading, he should make his own "spot test" of library use and make known to the faculty how the typical student presently meets the instructor's requirements and expectations.

NOTES

1. Henry M. Wriston, *Academic Procession; Reflections of a College President.* N.Y., Columbia University Press, 1959, p. 137.

—"For thirty years, therefore, I waged war on the reserve shelf—not to abolish it completely, but to keep it in scale and reduce its adverse effect upon the broader use of the library. The campaign had various degrees of success and failure. But if I were to begin all over again I should fight even harder. In 'real life,' as the commencement orators so often refer to the years after graduation, there is no reserve shelf. If we seek to make students into intellectual self-starters, we should inculcate, during college, the habits which will be useful thereafter."

2. The Dartmouth College Library, one of the first libraries to recognize the implications of "textbook" study on library use, incorporated study rooms in the Baker Library in the late twenties. Even so, its reading rooms have been crowded by students reading texts.—"What Is a Library?" Dartmouth College *Library Bulletin,* 1 (ns):46-7, April, 1958.

Blueprint for a College Library

IF THE POINTS made in the preceding talks are valid, one may conclude that there are college administrators who would find it advantageous to take stock of the use made of their libraries, the quality of the collections, and the prevailing policies and practices bearing on library administration. In order to facilitate such a stock-taking, I have attempted in this concluding chapter to summarize some of the recurring problems which must be dealt with if the library is to be helped in doing its work most effectively. There will be no attempt to repeat what has already been said although some repetition is inevitable. The summary is neither detailed nor complete. The objective is the development and maintenance of a good college library, and the means of reaching this end may vary according to the times and the conditions under which they are applied.

I should like to believe that most administrators and faculty members will regard as self-evident what I have to say in the following pages; however, my visits to college campuses and libraries confirm an impression that in many instances I am describing things as they should be instead of as they are. Some of my recommendations are probably no better than hopes even though they are set forth here as essentials.

THE ADMINISTRATOR LEADS THE WAY

One may argue with some plausibility that the principal deterrent to good library service is apathy—administrators who think of the library merely as a distributing center for books, faculty members who are comfortably concerned with their own affairs, and librarians who have accustomed themselves to limitations and who hesitate to speak out for library needs for fear of getting into the administrators' hair. Apathy may be transformed into enthusiasm and effective action if administrators are genuinely interested in the library and convinced that they cannot afford to neglect its support, and if faculty and librarians have definite ideas about what needs to be done.

THE MUSEUM CONCEPT

The college library is not a storage house or a museum living a kind of Cinderella existence—sporadically financed, understaffed, and with a book collection made up from the attic discards of its friends. Rather, the library is an expensive instrument of instruction which must contain all the materials likely to be needed by the faculty, be properly housed, and adequately staffed by men and women who are no less able and intelligent than the teaching faculty. The use of its facilities must be pressed to the limit by the faculty.

BASIS OF SMOOTH OPERATION

Normally the librarian is appointed by the president and given the responsibility of formulating and administering library policies, rules, and regulations in order to secure the fullest use of the library by students and faculty. In order to do this job well, the librarian must have authority as well as responsibility. If the president clearly defines the librarian's authority, it will be a tremendous help to him in rendering a distinctive and invaluable library service. The definition of authority should include a statement describing (1) what types of materials purchased by the college belong to the library, (2) the librarian's authority and responsibility for acquiring and administering these materials, including their location and control, (3) the status of the librarian and professional staff members in the academic community, and (4) the selection, term of office, and principal functions of the library committee.[1] The importance of having such a code of library policy is discussed at length in an earlier chapter entitled "The College Administration and the Library" (p. 20-33).

The library's chief concern is with the instructional program of the college. The president will help it perform that function as it should if he sees to it that the librarian is appointed to such educational and administrative committees of the college as will enable him to keep well informed about academic and administrative policy, including matters relating to curriculum, buildings, planning, budget, and development.

DEPARTMENTAL LIBRARIES

The problem of departmental libraries on the college campus is constant, like sex in dormitory discussions. The principal argument for the departmental library is its *convenience* for those who use it in the department. This advantage is real when the information sought from the departmental library is factual, is needed at once, and does not require reference to the holdings of the college library. As against this advantage, there are serious disadvantages created by the short hours of opening, the cost of duplicating books and catalog and staff services, the frequent necessity of hunting up some member of the faculty if the departmental library is not properly staffed in order to get access to the collection, a hypercautious policy on the part of the department regarding loans to students and faculty in other departments, and a tendency toward proprietary attitudes on the part of the departmental faculty which may become so oppressive as to discourage others from going to the departmental collection. Studying the question exhaustively from the point of view of accessibility, cost, efficiency, adequacy, use of books, interrelationships of subject fields, and educational significance, Dr. Robert A. Miller concludes: "Approaching the problem . . . as realistically as possible, I cannot but conclude that centralization is the better policy for the college library." [2] Let it be clearly understood, however, that this conclusion is valid only if the collections are of high quality and readily accessible, if the librarians are vigorous and responsive to departmental needs, and if the book and reading space in the main library is not overcrowded. While only a few people will benefit from the departmental library collection, there are hundreds of students whose only chance to become acquainted with fields of knowledge outside their courses is through browsing among books and journals in the library. If the college library is truly an instrument of counter-specialization, then it is up to administrators and librarians who believe in broadening education to pursue its goals without compromise. The librarian should be broadminded enough, however, to recognize that there are situations, particularly in highly specialized subjects, where current periodicals and abstract literature may be housed usefully in the building where the department is located.

STAFFING

With the recruitment and replacement of librarians becoming more critical each year, it is important that the college secure, hold, and develop as many good staff members as possible. This is the head librarian's chief task and one in which he will need the firm backing of the president. Capable, conscientious, and perceptive librarians, who are supported by a sense of the importance of their work and a clear understanding of what they are supposed to be doing, are worth their weight in gold. The problem is how to recruit and hold them.

As to the source of staff, the natural place to turn is the library school. Graduate schools of librarianship, accredited by the American Library Association, are usually considered first (a list appears in the Appendix, p. 74-75). There are, however, colleges and universities in almost every state which offer a major in library science as part of their undergraduate curricula (*American Library Directory*, 23d ed., N.Y., Bowker, 1962, p. 971-91) and whose graduates are equipped to fill, and to fill well, subprofessional posts requiring a minimum of library training and experience. The American Library Association offers no placement services as such but provides a contact placement clearing-house at its annual meetings where employers may interview prospective candidates. Direct contact between the employer and the head librarians of colleges and universities in the region has proved effective as a recruiting measure. The personnel and advertising columns of such library journals as the *ALA Bulletin, College and Research Libraries, Wilson Library Bulletin,* and *Library Journal* are sometimes utilized for recruiting candidates.

Of all the problems involved in attracting bright young men and women to college librarianship, none is more difficult to surmount than the practice of using library posts as a dumping ground for ineffectual teachers, dependents of deceased professors, and the neurotic or frustrated to whom for one reason or another the college feels obligated. We are bound to emphasize this point because there is much evidence that those responsible for making appointments are not aware that librarianship is in fact a profession for which training is desirable, or of the quality and kind of training that is available.

In holding and developing the library staff, the administration should accept the principle that the librarians should have pay and prospects of similar quality to those of the teaching faculty, account being taken, of course, of the importance of their positions and of the scale of salaries provided for the various ranks of the instructional staff.[3] Where it exists, the gap between the salaries of the teaching faculty and librarians should be reduced.

The staff should be accorded the same privileges as the faculty with respect to tenure, retirement, insurance, and other fringe benefits. There should be a continuous urge to improve staff ability and for this purpose librarians should be eligible for leaves of absence for scholarly study and travel on the same basis as the faculty. Membership on faculty committees should be encouraged. Not only will this give the individual library staff member a sense of his value in the academic process, it will also assist him in seeing the library in academic perspective and enable him to work more meaningfully in collecting, organizing, and making readily available the facilities of print for use in teaching.

THE GIFT HORSE

Many college presidents and faculty members follow the adage, at least insofar as the library is concerned, that one should never look a gift horse in the mouth. Libraries attract gifts as a magnet attracts iron filings. The donor thinks his gifts are priceless; the chances are they are worthless. A book's value to a library is governed by three factors operating together: (1) its intrinsic worth, (2) its usefulness for specific curricular purposes, and (3) the extent to which the library already has adequate material on the subject. Gifts are not only expensive to process but they take up costly shelf space; they may also require special handling. As Keyes D. Metcalf so graphically demonstrated almost ten years ago when costs were lower than they are now, each gift journal cost his institution $.25 to record and "check in" and $3 to catalog, occupied space costing $1.50 to construct, and involved an additional expense of $1 endowment for maintenance—a total of $5.75 per volume.[4] While this figure is not cited to discourage gift giving, it is important that administrators and faculty recognize something of the costs involved when they deposit or encourage others to deposit their old copies of *Time* and *Life* on the library doorstep. Everyone in a position of academic responsibility has the obligation to see to it that the library collection is not weakened by the acceptance of useless gifts or those with restrictions which limit their usefulness and greatly add to the cost of library operation. Nor are library gifts confined to printed materials. Libraries are the frequent recipients of swords, medals, death masks, uniforms, buggy whips, and branding irons. The library is not a curio shop although some people would not hesitate to turn it into one.

No college, of course, can afford to be so bold as to state publicly that it will not accept gifts with strings attached any more than it can state publicly the circumstances under which it will not offer an honorary degree. But it should be possible to take a positive approach and state persuasively the library's need for gifts, the kinds of gifts which would prove valuable, and the terms which would enhance the value of gifts to the library.

FINANCES

The libraries in the leading colleges of the country, and in many institutions which would modestly make no claim to superiority, have developed notably during the past decade or two, and have established themselves as an indispensable element in the programs of their respective colleges. Even so, it would be idle to deny that there are many colleges in which library activity, and the appreciation of its importance, fall short of a satisfactory standard. The statistics of financial support published annually by the United States Office of Education leave no doubt on this score.

What are the principal requirements of the library budget? As a practical matter, what standards can the college administrator apply in gauging the adequacy of the library budget? The need for a continuing supply of new books and journals for course work is readily recognized. While there is no way of calculating exactly *what* supply of these materials is necessary for first-rate college work, the demand for current books and journals is constantly increasing because of the proliferation of courses and the increase in the production of printed matter in special subject fields. There is no reason to believe that either trend has reached its peak. Book prices, moreover, are rising so fast and so steadily that the college library needs an increase in its book funds each year just to stay even. So far we have mentioned only current materials; no library is so strong in its basic collection that it can afford to neglect annual purchases of older works. Unless the book budget provides sufficient funds for filling in gaps in the collection as well as for current materials, there will most assuredly be a decline both in the quality of the library and in classroom instruction.

Books are only part of the library cost. For every dollar the library spends on books it will need approximately two dollars for staffing. In spite of salary increases in recent years, the salaries of librarians are far from adequate and ought to be increased from present levels by at least fifty per cent. The competition among college, public, and school libraries is extremely stiff, and the personnel shortage is made even more critical by the demands for librarians from industry and government. Few colleges can compete in terms of salary with the special libraries of business and industry and fewer still with the Federal Government.

In judging the adequacy of the total library budget, library surveyors frequently use the following criteria: (1) the ratio of library expenditures to the general and educational expenditures of the college, (2) the per student expenditure for library service, and (3) comparison with the expenditures of libraries of colleges of similar size and program. Based on an analysis of actual expenditures over a number of years, the Association of College and Research Libraries' standards recommend "a minimum of 5 per cent of the total educational and general budget." [5] Where course offerings and enrollments are expanding rapidly and where courses leading to the master's degree are offered, the Association recommends a higher percentage, and it adds that special budgetary provision should be made for audio-visual materials and services if these are supplied by the library.

In determining an adequate per student expenditure for library service, Moran and Tolman calculated in 1951 that $50 per student was the minimum annual expenditure that would enable the library to do its work well.[6] The spiral of book prices and salary increases has continued unabated since then. An analysis of recent studies reveals that the average price of books and periodicals rose approximately 47 per cent between 1947-1949 and 1960 [7] while the salaries of librarians in fifteen leading colleges increased an average of 68 per cent for all ranks.[8] On the basis of these data, it is not difficult to calculate that library expenditures have risen 61 per cent since 1947-1949 and that the recommended standard of $50 per student in 1951 will have to be increased to $80 per student to provide a comparable quality of library service in 1962.

PHYSICAL FACILITIES

In talking to any good college administrator, one is soon made aware that his aim is to make his college one of the best in the state and the region. The president is clear and articulate about the need for a fine faculty. In the next breath, however, he is likely to be asking for advice on how to remodel and enlarge the library building, a structure already enlarged once and obsolete for modern library purposes the day it was built. The relationship between securing and holding a fine faculty and having a first-rate library is apparently overlooked. It is clear that librarians have failed to convince administrators of the consequences of inferior library quarters and collections. The importance of the library can hardly be overestimated.[9] Each department of the college contributes to the whole. A new fine arts building contributes to the teaching of the fine arts but the library building has a broader function. The library is the one central, all important building on the campus, making possible by the quality of its facilities, collections, and staff real college work by students and faculty alike. Without access to a

modern, adequate library, no college can hope to hold an outstanding faculty, or, in other words, genuinely be a college in any meaningful sense of the word.

Among the important criteria by which a good college library building can be judged are these: the nearness of the library site to the academic buildings; seating for a minimum of 30 per cent of the maximum projected enrollment excluding such special areas as pre-view rooms, seminars, and the like; and accommodation for growth in the book collection for the next twenty years. The building should provide the best in the essentials of good lighting, air-conditioning, and soundproofing. The interior arrangement should intermingle books with readers and provide open access to books and all forms of recorded knowledge. Research has shown that students strongly prefer small places for study where an individual can work alone or with one or two others.[10] The more colleges tend to develop and to require independence on the part of students, the greater will be the need for individual studies and small work spaces. Smokers should have separate accommodations. Readers should have access to a number of individual typing booths. A seminar or two should be provided for advanced class instruction requiring extensive use of bibliographical tools. Private studies may be needed for individual faculty members and visiting scholars. If audio-visual aids are serviced by the library, there will be need for a pre-viewing room as well as places for servicing, repairing, and storing them. A special collections room should accommodate rare books, college archives, and special materials, and at the same time provide for hospitality to visitors by having kitchenette facilities adjoining. While the building should be open, functional, and flexible, it need not be of the characterless factory type. By its proportions, intimate reading areas, variety of furnishings, and warm colors, it can offer an invitation to students and faculty to read and enjoy books.

These then are some of the recurring problems and needs of the college library. It may seem to the college administrator that I have said too much about his indeterminateness in these matters and not enough about the librarian's sins of omission. Not all librarians, it is true, possess an equal comprehension of the purposes and practices of librarianship. In the smaller colleges, especially, they are likely to be so overburdened with library routines that they are unable to comprehend clearly the library's relation to the college's purposes and teaching methods. Some librarians, unfortunately, are more interested in the mechanics of librarianship than in educational processes and results; others are so anxious to please everybody that they lose any sense of discrimination between the important and the trivial. However, this criticism is not quite the point. In this book the matter of concern is the administrator's relation to the library. Speaking as a librarian, and for librarians, I am asserting simply that the college library must have a fair chance to do what it is intended to do before the college can genuinely educate. No problem of college administration—the liberal arts and the professional, general education and specialization, faculty participation in college administration, nonacademic activities of students, or automobile parking—is more important than raising the library to the position of prominence on the campus which it ought to occupy as "the heart of the college." If the college administrator is articulate about what the library is supposed to do, if he defines clearly the authority and responsibility of the librarian, if he urges the faculty to make the library one of its chief concerns, and if he seeks adequate financial support for building strong collections and a good staff, I believe the college library will have possibilities for educational development far beyond any that are now recognized.

NOTES

1. Eugene H. Wilson, "Government and control of the college library." *In:* H. H. Fussler, ed., *The Function of the Library in the Modern College.* Chicago, University of Chicago Graduate Library School, 1954. p. 22-36.

2. Robert Miller, "Centralization versus Decentralization." *ALA Bulletin,* 33:75-9, 134-5, February, 1939.

3. It is worth noting in this connection that the American Association of University Professors does not regard "teaching" as being limited to "the formal conducting of a course" and recognizes that "librarians of professional status are engaged in teaching or research."—*AAUP Bulletin,* 42:180, Spring, 1956.

4. Keyes D. Metcalf, *Report of the Harvard University Library* . . . . Cambridge, Mass., Harvard University Library, 1955, p. 15.

5. "Standards for College Libraries." *College and Research Libraries,* 20:274-80, July, 1959 (reprinted in the Appendix of this book, p. 76-86).

6. Virginia L. Moran and Mason Tolman, "College Library Study." *Library Journal,* 76:907, November 15, 1951.

7. *The Cost of Library Materials: Price Trends of Publications,* by Frank L. Schick and William H. Kurth. Washington, D.C., U.S. Office of Education, 1961 (OE-15029A), p. 11, 14-15.

8. Based on a comparison of salaries of librarians, library department heads, and "other professional assistants" of 15 leading colleges: *College and Research Libraries,* 13:68-81, January, 1952; *Library Statistics of Colleges and Universities.* Washington, D.C., U.S. Office of Education, 1962 (OE-15023-61).

9. Probably the most important step the president can take in planning a new building or enlargement is to secure the advice of a librarian with rich building experience and/or a library-architect specialist. At the beginning stage in planning the president or his librarian should identify members of the library profession who are expert in building matters and secure their assistance on a consultant basis. Some librarians in colleges may hesitate to raise questions with their presidents about consultants because of the expense but such an attitude is penny wise and pound foolish.

10. Committee for New College, *Student Reactions to Study Facilities, with Implications for Architects and College Administrators.* Amherst, Mass., Amherst College, 1960.

Appendix

SURVEY OF LIBRARY USE *

We need your cooperation and assistance in obtaining as complete an estimate as possible of the daily use made of the Library. Please give thoughtful and careful attention to the questions listed below, and return the questionnaire to the Control Desk attendant before leaving the Library. We ask that you fill out a questionnaire each time you come to the Library today, even though you may have filled out one on previous trips. Your answers will help us to improve library service and to make the Library more useful to you. Do not sign your name.

1. Reasons for coming to the Library this trip (check only those applicable)
   a. To return, charge out, or renew books _____
   b. To read Reserve books in the Reserve Reading Room _____
   c. To do assigned reading in library materials other than Reserve books _____
   d. To look up material for a paper, report, thesis, and so forth _____
   e. For general reading not assigned in class _____
   f. To study own books _____
   g. Other reasons (specify)

2. Materials used in Library this trip (Do not count books you charge out for use outside the Library)
   a. Number of books, journals, newspaper volumes from the main book stacks _____
   b. Number of books from the Browsing Room collection _____
   c. Number of government publications from the Documents Center collection _____
   d. Number of reference books from the Reference Room collection _____
   e. Number of books from the Reserve Room collection _____
   f. Number of books and journals from the Science Library collection _____
   g. Number of current periodicals in Current Periodical Room _____
   h. Number of current newspapers in Current Periodical Room _____
   i. Number of library microfilms, microcards, microprints _____
   j. Number of items in Special Collections Department (manuscripts, maps, rare books, etc.) _____
   k. Number of phonograph records in Music Listening Room _____

3. Your status (check one)
   a. Freshman _____   e. Graduate student _____
   b. Sophomore _____   f. Faculty _____
   c. Junior _____   g. Staff (other than library) _____
   d. Senior _____   h. Other (specify) _____

Have you turned in another library use questionnaire today? Yes_____ No_____

* Source: Guy R. Lyle, *The Administration of the College Library*, 3d ed. N.Y., H. W. Wilson Company, 1961, p. 407.

ACCREDITED LIBRARY SCHOOLS
AMERICAN LIBRARY ASSOCIATION *

Atlanta University School of Library Service, Atlanta, Ga. Est. 1941

University of *California* School of Librarianship, Berkeley. Est. 1919

University of *California* at *Los Angeles* School of Library Service. Est. 1960

Catholic University of America Department of Library Science, Washington, D.C. Est. 1938

University of *Chicago* Graduate Library School, Chicago, Ill. Est. 1928

Columbia University School of Library Service, New York, N.Y. Est. 1887

Texas Woman's University School of Library Science, *Denton*. Est. 1929

University of *Denver* Graduate School of Librarianship, Denver, Colo. Est. 1931

Drexel Institute of Technology Graduate School of Library Science, Philadelphia, Pa. Est. 1891

Emory University Division of Librarianship, Atlanta, Ga. Est. 1905

Florida State University Library School, Tallahassee. Est. 1947

University of *Illinois* Graduate School of Library Science, Urbana. Est. 1893

Indiana University Division of Library Science, Bloomington. Est. 1949

University of *Kentucky* Department of Library Science, Lexington. Est. 1933

Louisiana State University Library School, Baton Rouge. Est. 1931

McGill University Library School, Montreal, Quebec, Canada. Est. 1927 †

University of *Michigan* Department of Library Science, Ann Arbor. Est. 1926

University of *Minnesota* Library School, Minneapolis. Est. 1928

University of *North Carolina* School of Library Science, Chapel Hill. Est. 1931

University of *Oklahoma* School of Library Science, Norman. Est. 1929

---

* "Accredited Library Schools." *ALA Membership Directory, 1961*. Chicago, A.L.A., 1962, p. 439; *ALA Bulletin*, November, 1962, p. 938-9.

† Basic program at the fifth-year level leading to the professional bachelor's degree accredited under Standards for Accreditation adopted by the A.L.A. Council, July 13, 1951.

George Peabody College for Teachers *Peabody* Library School, Nashville, Tenn. Est. 1928

Pratt Institute Library School, Brooklyn, N.Y. Est. 1890

Rosary College Department of Library Science, River Forest, Ill. Est. 1930

Rutgers University Graduate School of Library Service, New Brunswick, N.J. Est. 1953

Simmons College School of Library Science, Boston, Mass. Est. 1902

University of *Southern California* School of Library Science, Los Angeles. Est. 1936

Syracuse University School of Library Science, Syracuse, N.Y. Est. 1908

University of *Texas* Graduate School of Library Science, Austin. Est. 1948

University of *Toronto,* Ontario College of Education Library School, Toronto, Ontario, Canada. Est. 1928 †

University of *Washington* School of Librarianship, Seattle. Est. 1911

Western Michigan University Department of Librarianship, Kalamazoo. Est. 1945

Western Reserve University School of Library Science, Cleveland, Ohio. Est. 1904

University of *Wisconsin* Library School, Madison. Est. 1906

STANDARDS FOR COLLEGE LIBRARIES *

These standards are designed to provide a guide for the evaluation of libraries in American colleges and universities which emphasize four-year undergraduate instruction and may or may not have graduate programs leading to a Master's degree. They are not applicable, however, to junior college libraries nor to libraries of academic institutions stressing advanced research. For simplicity's sake, the term "college library" is used throughout rather than a long phrase such as "library in a college or university granting Bachelors' or Bachelors' and Masters' degrees."

I. FUNCTIONS OF THE COLLEGE LIBRARY

The college library should be the most important intellectual resource of the academic community. Its services, given by a competent staff of adequate size, should be geared to implement the purposes of the college's general program and to meet the specific educational objectives of the institution. Its collections should aim at presenting the heritage of Western and Eastern thought in all its richness, but should stress those particular areas which are central to the curriculum of the institution. No artificial barriers should separate the library from the classroom or the library staff from the teaching faculty. Beyond supporting the instructional program to the fullest extent, the library should endeavor to meet the legitimate demands of all its patrons, from the senior professor engaged in advanced research to the freshman just entering upon the threshold of higher learning, to stimulate and encourage the student to develop the lifelong habit of good reading, and to play its proper role in the community and in the wider realm of scholarship beyond the campus.

The standards laid down in this document must always be interpreted in the light of the aims and needs of the institution of which the library is a part.

* Source: *College and Research Libraries*, 20:274-80, July, 1959. The statement was prepared by the Association of College and Research Libraries Committee on Standards, Felix E. Hirsch, chairman. Footnotes included in the original document have been omitted. Copies of the statement are obtainable from the Association of College and Research Libraries, 50 East Huron Street, Chicago 11, Illinois.

II. STRUCTURE AND GOVERNMENT

If the institution's board of control has a committee on the library, its duties and authority should be clearly defined, and the relationship of the librarian to the committee should be stated. The committee should be concerned with general library policy and not with matters of an administrative and executive nature.

The librarian should be directly responsible to the president. Since the library is an important department serving the entire institution, the librarian should rank with other chief administrative officers. However, since he is concerned primarily with the academic program of the institution, he will work in a particularly close relationship with the head of the academic program. The librarian should be a member of the college planning group for the curriculum and of any other committee whose activities will vitally affect the future of library service.

As a rule, there should be a faculty library committee. The committee should act strictly in an advisory capacity. It should consist of both senior and junior faculty members, carefully chosen for their demonstrated understanding of library problems and for their willingness to take a genuine interest in the collections beyond those pertaining to their own departments. The committee should intrepret the problems and policies of the library to the faculty and, in turn, make suggestions for the improvement of library service. It may also represent the faculty in the apportionment of book funds, insofar as they are allocated to the departments. The librarian should be a regular member of the committee and may serve as its chairman.

Wherever circumstances permit, a student committee on the library should be established to provide for a better liaison with the student body. Such a committee should be carefully selected and its functions properly defined; it should work closely with the librarian.

The librarian should always be entrusted with planning and administering the library budget. No action affecting the library finances should be taken by administrative officers of the college without prior consultation with the librarian. All materials purchased from library funds or books and periodicals otherwise acquired by the institution should be considered a part of the library and should be under the control of the librarian.

The organization of the library should be logical and suitable to the institution. Lines of authority should be clearly drawn and should not cross. While the librarian must assume responsibility for the administration of the library, he should seek the advice of members of his staff on important matters of policy and procedure. Channels of communication within the staff should be well defined and generally understood.

The librarian must keep such statistical records as are necessary to give a clear picture of the activities, acquisitions, and use of the library. He should keep and regularly report statistics as requested by the United States Office of Education, regional accrediting agencies, and the Association of College and Research Libraries.

III. BUDGET

The funds provided for the support of the library will in large measure determine the quality of the library resources and services. The library's holdings, the prevailing methods of instruction, the size of faculty and student body, the extent to which the college encourages and provides for individual study, and the variety of graduate offerings are factors which influence the budgetary needs of the library.

The library budget should be determined in relation to the total budget of the institution for educational and general purposes. ["Edutional and general" is defined by the United States Office of Education as operating funds used to defray expenditures for administration, instruction, research, extension services, plant operation and maintenance, and organized activities related to instructional departments.] The program of library service outlined in these standards will normally require a minimum of 5 per cent of the total educational and general budget. The percentage must be higher if the library's holdings are seriously deficient, if there is rapid expansion in student population or course offerings, or if the institution fosters a wide range of studies at the Master's level or programs of independent study. While the allocation of library funds for specific purposes will depend on the needs of the individual institution, experience shows that a good college library usually spends twice as much (or more) for salaries as it does for books.

It should be considered a serious danger signal by the college authorities if the library budget sinks appreciably below the median ratio of library expenditures to total educational and general institutional expenditures for comparable institutions as indicated in the latest annual college library statistics.

IV. STAFF

The library should be operated by a broadly educated and highly qualified staff of professional librarians, under the direction of a chief librarian. The professional librarian is defined as one holding a graduate library degree.

The size of the staff will vary with the size of the institution, but three professional librarians constitute the minimum number required for effective service, i.e., the chief librarian and the staff members responsible for readers' services and technical processes. In addition to student enrollment, several other factors are important in determining the number of librarians needed, such as the type of organization within the library, the size and character of the collections, the teaching methods prevailing in the institution, the number of hours during which the library is open, and the arrangement of the building. At least one professional librarian should be on duty at all times during which the library is open for full service.

In addition to the professional librarians, the library should have an adequate non-professional staff. The ratio of professional to non-professional staff will vary according to the specific needs of institutions. Great care should be taken that professional staff members do not spend their time in doing work that is essentially of a clerical nature. Student assistants may be employed effectively in a variety of tasks, but, as a rule, they cannot be expected to perform the same kind of indispensable services that competent clerical workers will.

As the size of the library increases, the ratio of the non-professional to the professional staff should be larger. While it may be impossible to have uniform standards for the size of the staff, attention should be called to the formulas designed in certain states, which appear to present reasonable patterns within which most institutions can develop their programs of library service. Professional librarians should have faculty status, with the benefits enjoyed by the teaching staff. These should include such items as tenure, sick leave, liberal vacations, an adequate retirement plan, and sabbaticals. The salary schedule for librarians should be the same as for teaching members of the faculty. It follows that librarians—in line with the established promotion policies at their institution—should be expected to do graduate work in such areas as would contribute to their effectiveness in their respective positions. In some instances such a program of study might well lead to a second or third Master's degree rather than to a Ph.D. degree.

Opportunity should be granted for engaging in such studies. However, provision should also be made for giving recognition through promotion or salary increase to exceptional ability in the performance of duties.

The library staff should take an active part in the instructional program of the institution. Specific provision should be made for formal instruction in the use of the library, possibly in collaboration with academic departments. The participation of the staff will also include informal individual instruction in the use of the library, advice to faculty members on bibliographical matters, work on various committees, and the preparation of reading lists and special reports regarding library facilities or services. Such activities are part of the normal operation of a college library. Staff members with appropriate subject background may also help to bridge the gap between the library and the classroom by teaching a course in a subject area.

Members of the library staff must be chosen with great care, since they are to perform such a variety of important educational functions. The chief librarian in particular "needs the skill to direct a highly complex organization well, but his thinking and planning must be that of a teacher and scholar. . . . He must know what scholarship is and what teaching entails. He must demonstrate the competence to merit the respect of his colleagues as an educator."

V. LIBRARY COLLECTIONS

A. *Books and Periodicals*

The library's collection of books, periodicals, pamphlets, documents, newspapers, maps, microfilm, microcards, microprint, and other materials, must be so constituted and organized as to give effective strength and support to the educational program of the institution. The collection should meet the full curricular needs of undergraduate students and should be easily accessible to them. It should provide properly for the demands of graduate students in each field in which the institution offers the Master's degree. Also it should contain a generous selection of works to keep the members of the faculty abreast of the latest advances in modern scholarship and to assist them in their professional growth. If special programs of independent study involving a wide use of books are carried on, provision must be made for them in the library's collection.

80

In addition to the materials related directly or indirectly to the curriculum, the collection should contain the standard works which represent the heritage of civilization. These works should be continuously suppplemented by a wide variety of books which combine timeliness with enduring value, chosen to arouse the intellectual curiosity of students and to satisfy their recreational reading needs.

There should be a strong and up-to-date reference collection consisting of the most authoritative reference works and bibliographies in all major fields of knowledge. This collection must not be restricted to subjects which form part of the curriculum, nor to publications in the English language.

The periodicals subscription list should be well balanced and carefully chosen to meet the requirements of students for collateral course reading, to provide in some measure for the research needs of advanced students and faculty, to keep the faculty informed of developments in their fields, and to afford thought-provoking general and recreational reading. Newspaper subscriptions should provide news coverage at the national, regional, and local levels; they should include also one or more leading papers from abroad. Various political points of view should be represented. It is essential that the major journals and newspapers be kept and bound systematically or preserved in microtext form.

Printed, manuscript, and archival materials pertaining to the institution of which the library is a part should be collected and preserved.

The right of the librarian to select books and other materials representing all sides of controversial issues must be safeguarded by the institution, and any attempts at censorship from whatever sources or for whatever reasons must be resisted.

The quality of the library collections should not be sacrificed to unnecessary duplication of titles. However, works of lasting significance or of contemporary importance should be available in a sufficient number of copies to give students a fair opportunity to examine them thoroughly.

Obsolete materials, such as outmoded books, superseded editions, incomplete sets of longer works, broken files of unindexed journals, superfluous duplicates, and worn out or badly marked volumes, should be continuously weeded, with the advice of faculty members concerned. Gifts should be accepted only in case they add to the strength of the library collections and do not carry unreasonable restrictions. President, faculty, and librarian should join in developing a policy which clearly defines what kinds of gifts are desirable for the institution and why it is important educationally to integrate them with the regular collections except in rare instances.

If funds are allocated to departments, a substantial portion beyond fixed costs for periodicals and continuations should be reserved for direct assignment by the librarian. This portion should be large enough to provide for the purchase of reference works, general publications, expensive sets, books for recreational reading, and works which cross departmental lines, as well as for correcting weaknesses in the library's collection.

Library holdings should be checked frequently against standard bibliographies, both general and subject, as a reliable measure of their quality. A high percentage of listed titles which are relevant to the program of the individual institution, should be included in the library collections.

The size of the library collections is largely determined by the following major factors: (1) The extent and nature of the curriculum, (2) the number and character of graduate programs, (3) the methods of instruction, (4) the size of the undergraduate and graduate student body, both full-time and extension, and (5) the need of the faculty for more advanced materials which cannot be met conveniently by the use of research libraries in the area.

An analysis of small college library statistics suggests that no library can be expected to give effective support to the instructional program if it contains fewer than 50,000 carefully chosen volumes. A steady growth is essential to any good college library. The rate of growth of the library collection may slow down, however, when the number of volumes reaches approximately 300,000. Since there appears to be a correlation between the growth of the student body and the growth of the collection, there is a convenient measure based upon observation of the development of college libraries, which may serve as a guide: up to 600 students, 50,000 volumes; for every additional 200 students, 10,000 volumes. Part-time and extension students should be equated into full-time student figures for the purpose of such computations. It is, however, clearly understood, that these are minimal figures and that stronger institutions will demand considerably larger and richer collections.

The library's collections should be fully organized for use. The main catalog of the library should serve as a union catalog for all collections of the library whether housed in the main building or in college departments. The catalog should follow the Library of Congress and American Library Association cataloging codes as standards. Materials should be classified according to an accepted scheme in general usage and be subject to continual editing to keep the catalog abreast of modern technological developments. The catalog should also be constantly revised to keep it up-to-date in terminology.

B. *Audio-Visual Materials*

Audio-visual materials including films, filmstrips, recordings, and tapes are an integral part of modern instruction, and every college library must concern itself with them. The library should take the initiative for providing them, if no other agency on campus has been assigned this responsibility.

If the library is handling the program, it should be enabled to do so by special budgetary provisions, including those for additional staff. The program must be, both in its budget and its operation, an integral part of the whole of the library's functions. No audio-visual program can succeed without adequate facilities for the use of equipment and materials.

The librarian is bound by the same high standards of selection for films and recordings that he uses for books.

VI. BUILDING

Successful library service presupposes an adequate library building. The college library building should be centrally located and functionally designed. The type of building provided will depend on the character and the aims of the institution, but it should always meet the general demands of efficient operation. The residential college will have different building requirements from the college which serves commuters only. Every new building plan should include provisions for future expansion.

The size of the library building will depend on the type and size of institution which it serves, the instructional methods employed, the character of the collections and the number of volumes. In general, the seating capacity of a new building should be based on the anticipated growth over a twenty-year period. Accommodations for at least one third of the student body will be essential. The changing concept of the role of the library in the academic community may make necessary an upward revision of this figure. Any particular situation will be further affected by the availability of other study facilities on campus.

Provision should be made for expansion of reading areas where students may have easy access to books and other materials. Book space, too, must be ample not only for the present, but for the foreseeable future as well. On principle, shelf space in a new building should be planned so that it allows at least for a doubling of the collection. Adequate housing must also be provided for special materials such as current issues of periodicals, maps, pictures, art books, films, records, and microtexts.

Well-planned areas must be provided for any and all services which the library undertakes to furnish, e.g., well-arranged general circulation and reference areas, display space, rooms for listening to recordings, faculty studies, etc.

The efficient operation of the library also entails adequate quarters for the processes of ordering, preparation, cataloging, binding and mending, filing, and similar activities. Staff work-areas should comprise at least 125 square feet of floor space per person. Persons holding administrative positions should be given sufficient private office space. A staff lounge with simple kitchen facilities is highly desirable for the convenience of staff and visitors.

Much of the building's effectiveness depends on proper provisions for heat, light, and air. Sound-conditioning, air-conditioning, lighting, and decoration should be carefully planned so that students and faculty are encouraged to study in a cheerful and comfortable atmosphere. The proper control of humidity and heat should also be provided for books and materials, especially those that are rare and valuable.

College libraries should be equipped with well-designed library furniture of high quality. A variety of types of seating should be available including tables, carrels, individual desks, and comfortable lounge chairs away from tables. The table space of 3 x 2 feet per reader is recommended for general library use.

VII. THE QUALITY OF THE SERVICE AND ITS EVALUATION

In the field of librarianship, probably nothing is more difficult than assessing the quality of a college library, since it involves so many intangible factors. However, nothing is more important than to know how effective the library service actually is.

One way to measure the success of library activities is a continuous careful evaluation of the statistical records of the circulation department. Where the library has open shelves, these records will give only part of the picture. It is likely, however, that the library service to students is improving if the per capita figures of books on regular loan (two weeks or longer) to students show an upward trend over a considerable period of time. Surveys of what students are actually reading in the library at a given time, studies of books not supplied, reference questions not answered, and the character of interlibrary loans are additional bases for evaluating book collection and service. Such statistical investigations, however, must be made with caution and with full consideration of all factors involved. Much will depend on the teaching methods employed by the faculty. Therefore, it is particularly important to keep faculty members regularly informed on new publications, new acquisitions, etc. The librarian should work closely with them, as they plan new courses and develop new educational ideas, and assist them in gauging the actual and potential significance of the library resources for the teaching in their fields. The effectiveness of the instruction in the use of the library given by the staff will be reflected in how well the students avail themselves of the library resources.

Another approach is an evaluation of the library resources and services undertaken jointly by the teaching faculty and the library staff after careful planning. Such a self-evaluation should always lead to the strengthening of the ties between classroom and library. It is recommended that such self-studies be undertaken frequently. When necessary, the advice of outside experts should be secured.

VIII. INTERLIBRARY COOPERATION

By the nature of his work, the college librarian has to think, above all, of serving the faculty and students at his institution. But he should not lose sight of the important benefits to be derived from pooling the resources of his library with those of other interested libraries in the same community, region, state, and in the nation. This will have two

85

salutary results. First, "it will greatly help the participating libraries to provide for their readers the broad and rich intellectual opportunities to which they are entitled." Second, such planned collaboration will make each dollar spent by cooperating libraries "go further than it would go if spent by an individual library."

In particular, the college library should cooperate with other college, university, school and public library agencies in the community and the neighboring area for reference service to readers beyond the campus.

The librarian should investigate the possibility of cooperation with other libraries in the area, e.g., for the planned purchasing of materials to avoid unnecessary duplication and to increase the resources available to each cooperating library. On the other hand, the library should not seek to borrow from other libraries materials which are basic to the college program.

In conclusion, it should be remembered that American higher education has entered upon an era of momentous change. These standards should be interpreted by college librarians and their authorities in a spirit that will enable the college libraries of the nation not only to maintain but to strengthen their position in the face of this new challenge.

Index

This index includes citations to authors and titles only when they are named in the text.

Academic image of the librarian. Kevin Guinagh, 11-19
Academic qualifications of librarian, 15
Accredited library schools, 74-5
Acquisition program
  effect of library goals on, 40-1
  importance of effective organization in, 43-4
  principles of selection in, 35-41
Administrator. *See* College president
American Association of University Professors, cited, 16; on librarians and teaching, 69, note 3
The American College President. H. W. Stoke, cited, 23
American Library Directory, 23d ed., cited, 62
Architecture and building, 66-7
Association of College and Research Libraries. *Standards,* 76-86

Bishop, W. W., quoted, 36
Book collections
  See also Acquisition program
  budgetary provision, 48-50
  deterrents to quality growth, 35-9
  faculty contribution, 45-6
  librarian's role, 44-5
  library staff's role, 46-8
  types of materials, 42-3
Book lists, 38-9

Book losses, 14
Books, overdue. *See* Overdue books
Boyd, Julian, quoted, 22
Budget
  book funds, 48-9, 64-5
  criteria for determining adequacy, 65
  per student cost, 66

College president
  definition of librarian's role, 24-5, 59-60
  facilitating communication, 25-6
  librarian's relation to, 21-4
Communications, 25-9
Costs
  acquisition and cataloging, 63
  per student, 66
  record of gross costs, 65

Departmental libraries, 60-1

Faculty
  relations with librarian, 11-17, 29
  responsibility in book selection, 45-6
  student use of the library, 55-6
Finance. *See* Budget; Costs

Gifts, 63-4
Goodrich, N. L., quoted, 27
Government of the library, 24-5, 59-60

Guinagh, Kevin. Academic image of the librarian, 11-19

Librarian
    academic image of, 11-19
    authority delegated by president to, 24-5, 59-60
    isolation of from mainstream of campus life, 17, 27
    library-administrative relations, 20-9
    library-faculty relations, 26-9
    recruitment and selection of, 61-3, 74-5
Library building. *See* Architecture and building
Library goals, 40-1, 59
Library schools. *See* Accredited library schools
Library statistics, 64, 69, note 8

Metcalf, K. D., cited, 63
Miller, R. A., quoted, 61
Moran, V. L., cited, 66

Overdue books, 13-14

Physical facilities. *See* Architecture and building
The Popular Image of the Library and the Librarian, cited, 15
Professors. *See* Faculty

Recruitment of staff. *See* Staff
Reserve books, quoting H. M. Wriston, 56-7, note 1

Size of collections, unimportance of, 35-6
Spargo, J. W., quoted, 38
Staff
    recruitment and selection of, 61-3, 74-5
    responsibility in administrative-faculty relations, 29-32
    responsibility in book selection, 46-8
    status, 31-2, 62-3
Standards for College Libraries. Association of College and Research Libraries, 76-86
Statistics, library. *See* Library statistics
Stoke, H. W., quoted, 23
Study hall
    defeats library purpose, 18
    provision for, 55-6
    use of library as, 53-4
Survey of library use (form), 73

Taylor, Garland, quoted, 29
Tolman, Mason, cited, 66

United States Office of Education, cited, 64
United States Quarterly Book Review, cited, 39
Use of library
    implications of library use study, 55-6
    nature of library use, 52-5
    records (form), 73